BAPTISTS AND RELIGIOUS LIBERTY

The Freedom Road

A BAPTIST DOCTRINE AND HERITAGE STUDY FOR LIFE TODAY

William M. Pinson, Jr.

BAPTISTWAYPRESS®

Dallas, Texas

BAPTISTWAY PRESS® Management Team
Executive Director, Baptist General Convention of Texas: Randel Everett
Director, Missions, Evangelism, and Ministry Team: Wayne Shuffield
Ministry Team Leader: Phil Miller
Publisher, BAPTISTWAY PRESS®: Ross West

Cover and Interior Design and Production: Desktop Miracles, Inc.
Printer: Data Reproductions Corporation
Cover Image: Inscription in *A Short Declaration of the Mystery of Iniquity* by Thomas Helwys to King James of England in 1612; from Southern Baptist Historical Library and Archives. See page 6 for the text.

This book is one of a series of books produced in cooperation with the Baptist Distinctives Council/Texas Baptist Heritage Center of the Baptist General Convention of Texas—Executive Director Emeritus, BGCT, and volunteer Director, Texas Baptist Heritage Center, William M. Pinson, Jr.; volunteer Director of Organization and Communication, Doris A. Tinker; Chair of Baptist Distinctives Council, Royce Measures.

First edition: October 2007. Second printing: July 2008.
ISBN–13: 978–1–934731–00–0
ISBN–10: 1–934731–00–5

*This book is dedicated to the multitude of
persons who suffered fiendish torture,
horrible imprisonment, and
excruciating death to provide the
religious freedom we enjoy in the United States.*

About This Doctrine, Heritage, and Life Study

This book—*Baptists and Religious Liberty: The Freedom Road*—is one of a series of books on Baptist doctrine and heritage that BAPTISTWAY PRESS® is producing annually.[1] These studies are intended both for individual reading and study and for group studies in churches and other settings.

The intent of this series is to provide guidance in considering, understanding, and acting on some of our deeply-held Baptist beliefs, particularly as these beliefs intersect with current life. The intent is *not* to produce an official statement about these Baptist beliefs. Even to attempt to do so would go against the very nature of who Baptists are.

So, as you read and study this book and the other studies in the series, be prepared to think seriously and carefully. Engage the ideas with your own thought and study, especially of the Bible.

In addition to this study book, suggestions for teaching this study are available in *Baptists and Religious Liberty: The Freedom Road—Teaching Guide*. See www.baptistwaypress.org for additional resources for this and other studies produced by BAPTISTWAY PRESS®.

The Writer: William M. Pinson, Jr.

William M. Pinson, Jr., has served as executive director of the Executive Board of the Baptist General Convention of Texas; president, Golden Gate Baptist Theological Seminary; pastor, First Baptist Church, Wichita Falls, Texas; and professor, Southwestern Baptist Theological Seminary. Dr. Pinson is currently the executive director emeritus of the Baptist General Convention of Texas; distinguished visiting professor of Baylor University; distinguished university professor of Dallas Baptist University; and the volunteer director of the Texas Baptist Heritage Center.

Baptists and Religious Liberty

Text of Inscription on Front Cover

The inscription on the front cover is from *A Short Declaration of the Mystery of Iniquity* by Thomas Helwys to King James of England in 1612.[2] The book was the first document written in English that called for complete religious freedom.

> *Hear, O king, and despise not the counsel of the poor, and let their complaints come before thee. The king is a mortal man and not God, therefore has no power over the immortal souls of his subjects, to make laws and ordinances for them, and to set spiritual lords over them. If the king has authority to make spiritual lords and laws, then he is an immortal God and not a mortal man. O king, be not seduced by deceivers to sin against God whom you ought to obey, nor against your poor subjects who ought and will obey you in all things with body, life, and goods, or else let their lives be taken from the earth. God save the king.*
>
> — THO. HELWYS
> Spittalfield near London

Preface

WHEN REQUESTED TO WRITE THIS book, I agreed to do so out of a deep commitment to religious freedom and a strong desire to see Baptists continue to support it avidly so that the generations to come throughout the world might enjoy the fruits of freedom.

Many people were involved in making this book possible:

- A multitude of men and women sacrificed greatly to develop religious freedom in our country.

- Ross West, Publisher of BaptistWay Press®, provided helpful counsel, determined the length of the volume, and collaborated in defining its purpose and limits.

- Vester T. Hughes, Jr., provided both encouragement and resources that helped make available the materials needed for research.

- Bert Dominy, William Pitts, James Semple, and Brent Walker read all or part of the manuscript and made valuable suggestions.

- Doris Tinker, more than any other person, assisted in the project. Her superb research, editing, writing, and organizational skills contributed greatly. The daughter, sister, and mother of Baptist deacons; a former secretary to a pastor; and the Executive Associate in the office of Executive Director of the Baptist General Convention of Texas for twenty-seven years

before retiring and becoming Director of Organization and
Communication for the office of Executive Director Emeritus,
her understanding of and commitment to Baptist life runs deep.
Because of her huge contribution it is fitting that she share
authorship recognition, something that she firmly refused.

- Bobbie, my wife, provided encouragement in the long,
  time-consuming process of writing.

A few words about the nature of the book may be helpful to the
reader:

- The book focuses on the development of religious freedom in
  Europe and North America, not the entire world.

- It is a brief, non-technical summary, not a tome on sociology,
  history, political science, or theology as related to religious
  freedom. As such, experts in these various fields may find
  the material oversimplified. However, the book is not a
  comprehensive study but rather an introductory presentation.

- It deals primarily with the Baptist contributions to religious
  freedom and church-state separation while being grateful
  for the many others who have also helped to make religious
  liberty a reality.

- The goal of the book is to encourage and inspire Baptists
  and others to champion the struggle for religious liberty for
  all people *everywhere*. My hope and prayer is that this little
  volume will serve as a reminder of the price paid for the
  freedom we enjoy and help others to tell the story again and
  again of "the freedom road."

Introduction

PEOPLE IN THE UNITED STATES enjoy as great a degree of religious freedom as that found anywhere in the world.[1] Knowledgeable people of various nationalities and denominations have praised the Baptist role in providing such freedom.

- George Bancroft, an American historian in the 1800s, wrote, "Freedom of conscience, unlimited freedom of mind, was, from the first, the trophy of the Baptists."[2]
- The British historian Herbert S. Skeats stated, "It is the singular and distinguished honour of the Baptists to have repudiated, from their earliest history, all coercive power over the consciences and the actions of men with reference to religion."[3]
- The German historian-philosopher Georg Gottfried Gervinus in his *Introduction to the History of the Nineteenth Century*, in reference to the colony of Rhode Island founded by Baptists, observed, "Here in a little state the fundamental principles of political and ecclesiastical liberty practically prevailed before they were even taught in any of the schools of philosophy in Europe."[4]
- Frank S. Mead, a Methodist historian, declared of Baptists, "They are God's patriots, putting allegiance to Him always above allegiance to Caesar. Freedom of conscience and complete divorce of Church and State! How they have

suffered for that! They have faced mockery and mud, fines, whippings, and iron bars; they have been burned at the stake and pulled on the rack, but they have held to it."[5]

· William Warren Sweet, American historian, wrote, "But justice compels the admission that Jefferson's part in this accomplishment [of religious freedom] was not so great as was that of James Madison, nor were the contributions of either or both as important as was that of the humble people called Baptists."[6]

· Leo Pfeffer, jurist and church-state scholar, noted, "The Baptists were the most active of all the colonial religious bodies in their unceasing struggle for religious freedom and separation."[7]

· In 1884 Henry C. Vedder in *Baptists and Liberty of Conscience* wrote that the "glory of Baptists" was their fervent support of religious liberty for everyone.[8]

Baptists have trumpeted religious liberty long and loud and endured terrible persecution in order to help provide it for everyone, not just for themselves.

· John Smyth in his Confession of 1612 set forth one of the earliest statements on religious freedom, declaring that "Christ only is the king, and lawgiver of the church and conscience (James iv.12)."[9]

· Thomas Helwys, a Baptist pastor who died in prison for daring to declare to King James I that the Bible teaches freedom of religion, stated, "For men's religion to God is between God and themselves. The king shall not answer for it. Neither may the king be judge between God and man."[10]

· Edgar Young Mullins, a leading Baptist theologian of the early twentieth century, in 1908 wrote in *The Axioms of Religion*, "There has never been a time in their history, so far as that history is known to us, when they wavered in their doctrine of a free Church in a free State."[11]

- George W. Truett, in a sermon in 1920, declared about Baptists, "Their contention now is, and has been, and, please God, must ever be, that it is the natural and fundamental and indefeasible right of every human being to worship God or not, according to the dictates of his conscience, and, as long as he does not infringe upon the rights of others, he is to be held accountable alone to God for all religious beliefs and practices."[12]
- Baptist confessions of faith through the centuries have consistently advocated full religious freedom for all.[13]
- The First London Confession of 1644, often considered one of the most influential among Baptists, states, "And thus wee desire to give unto God that which is Gods, and unto *Cesar* that which is *Cesars*, and unto all men that which belongeth unto them, endevouring our selves to have always a cleare conscience void of offence towards God, and towards man."[14]
- A more recent Baptist confession, *The Baptist Faith and Message*, declares: "Church and state should be separate. . . . A free church in a free state is the Christian ideal, and this implies the right of free and unhindered access to God on the part of all men, and the right to form and propagate opinions in the sphere of religion without interference by the civil power."[15]

Religious freedom involves both a freedom *from* and a freedom *for*: freedom *from* efforts by either government or religious organizations to coerce religious beliefs or practices or to require support, financial or otherwise, of religion; freedom *for* the practice of religious convictions without interference from government or religious organizations as long as the practice does not harm the well-being of others. Such freedom has been bought with a terribly high price in human suffering and death.

Why have Baptists been praised for their role in the cause of religious liberty? Why have Baptists been in the forefront of the effort? Some answers to these questions will be found in the following pages. You are encouraged to read these pages not so much as a tranquil consideration of the past but as a clarion call to action in the present and the future.

> *"So if the Son sets you free,*
> *you will be free indeed."*
>
> **JOHN 8:36**

CHAPTER *One*

Traveling the Long Road to Freedom

> "Now who can hear Christ declare that his kingdom is
> NOT OF THIS WORLD, and yet believe that this blending of
> church and state together can be pleasing to him?"
>
> — ISAAC BACKUS[1]
> (1724–1806) Baptist pastor,
> Advocate for religious liberty

YOU JOIN A CROWD IN the public square, wondering what has attracted them. Pushing to the front of the group you see a man, stripped naked to the waist, tied cruelly to a pole, being beaten with a long whip with three cords. The big, burly man wielding the whip obviously is some sort of government-appointed executioner. From time to time he stops and spits on his hands to get a better grip. The sound of the whip ripping flesh from his back is met with determined silence by the victim. Twenty-five, twenty-six, twenty-seven times the whip lashes the bare back. Not even a whimper, much less a scream of pain, escapes him.

"Stand back," someone warns. "You will be spattered with blood!"

You ask, "What crime did he commit? How many lashes is he to receive?"

You are told, "He is a pastor and conducted a worship service not authorized by the government, and he taught doctrine not approved by the official church. He will get the maximum the law allows—thirty lashes."

❖　　❖　　❖

You pull your coat more closely around you as the autumn night brings a chill. When you pass the town jail you hear quiet sobbing from a woman inside. You shudder at the thought of being confined in a cold, damp, dark prison.

You ask a passerby, "Who is the woman inside? What did she do to deserve this treatment?"

The stranger answers, "She is a widow, a godly soul. All she did was refuse to pay the government required tax to support the official church, a church whose doctrines she does not believe. She's been there many days. Others, many as old, frail, and sick as she is, are being thrown in jail for not paying taxes to support a church whose doctrines they do not believe."

❖　　❖　　❖

You smell the pungent odor of burning sulfur as you approach the prison. As you move closer, you see that from behind the prison bars a young man stands preaching to the unruly crowd gathered. Through feverish lips he clearly proclaims the gospel.

You inquire of one in the crowd, "Who is he? What has he done? Why is there such a strong odor of sulfur?"

With a sneer, the man replies, "He is a preacher who dares preach without permission from the government. The stench of burning sulfur along with the rats, lice, dampness, and hunger he will not forget. And he will be in there for weeks."

❖　　❖　　❖

Where and when did these atrocities take place? You might think they occurred in some faraway country where religious freedom is unknown. No, they took place in America—when the land we term *the land of the free* knew little about religious freedom.

If you live in the United States today, the circumstance is much different. You can

- worship according to your beliefs without fear of government persecution
- belong to a church of your choice and not one the government controls
- support your church with tithes and offerings and not taxes
- share your faith without danger of arrest and imprisonment
- possess a Bible, read it openly, and interpret it personally
- choose not to believe in or practice any religion.

Only a few generations ago you would not have been free to do any of these. In many places in the world today this is still the case. Religious freedom is rare in much of the world. [2]

Yet, if you are like many people, you likely take such freedom for granted. Seldom do we pause to be grateful for freedom and for the sacrifices of those who have made it possible.

Religious freedom has come to us at a high price. Multiple thousands of people have suffered and died for the belief that all people should be free to exercise whatever religious faith they hold or even to hold no religious faith at all.

The people of no other nation enjoy more religious freedom than we do in the United States of America. Yet, ironically those who first settled here from Europe did not practice religious liberty. In fact, more than 200 years passed before full religious freedom became a reality.

"The freedom road" is long and difficult, marked by many, twists, turns, obstacles, and detours. Built by the sacrifice of a multitude of people over many centuries, it is marked by the blood of those who died that we might live in a land blessed with religious liberty.

Baptists played a significant part in building "the freedom road"— not just for themselves but for all people. Come, let's walk the road that led to religious freedom and meet many of these Baptists who made a difference, including those described in the opening incidents of this book.

The Beginnings

"The freedom road" begins literally at *the beginning*—at the beginning of the creation of the world and of humans. The Book of Genesis makes clear that God created man and woman with freedom—religious freedom. They were free to fellowship with God, to follow God's will—or not (Genesis 1:26–3:24). If God had wanted to create puppets, creatures with no ability to make choices, God could have done so. But God chose to create human beings with the freedom to choose. God told Adam, "You are free" (Gen. 2:16). Even after humankind sinned in disobedience to God, "God gives us both the privilege and the responsibility of choice."[3]

From the beginning the Bible indicates that God did not force his will on people. Thus for any individual or organization to endeavor to rob people of freedom by forcing them to worship God or by denying them the opportunity to fellowship with God according to the dictates of conscience is to thwart God's intent for human life. Freedom is a God-given right.

The Bible also indicates that freedom is a fearsome responsibility. Exercised in accord with God's will, it brings blessings. Used in violation of that will, it brings suffering. The Old Testament is filled with incidents illustrating these truths, beginning in the Garden of Eden with Adam and Eve. Obedience to God would have brought them life; disobedience brought death (Gen. 2:15–3:24).

God's gift of the Ten Commandments assumed the ability of people to understand them and the freedom to reject or accept them (see Exodus 20:1–17). With acceptance came blessing, but with rejection came punishment. Competence and freedom of choice were assumed. When Israel prepared to advance into the Promised Land, Joshua challenged the people, "Choose for yourselves this day whom you will serve" (Joshua 24:15). Such a challenge would have been meaningless if the people had no competency or freedom to choose. Freedom with accountability is a gift from God to human beings.

God intended people to be free to exercise their God-given competency. However, from early times efforts have been made to curtail religious freedom through persecution.

For example, in the Old Testament, King Nebuchadnezzar violated the religious freedom of his subjects by demanding they worship a golden idol. Shadrach, Meshach, and Abednego refused. The king had the three cast into a fiery furnace, where God protected them (Daniel 3:1–30). Later, King Darius demanded that all people worship in a certain way. Daniel refused to relinquish his religious freedom. He chose to disobey the king's law and worshiped the true God. As a result he was thrown into a den of lions, but God kept him from harm (Dan. 6:1–23). These followers of God were willing to suffer in order to exercise their God-given right to worship according to the dictate of conscience. They set an example of resisting efforts to crush religious freedom.

The New Testament Pattern

"The freedom road" passes through New Testament times. The New Testament record affirms religious freedom, but it also illustrates fierce efforts to eliminate it. In the first century the Roman Empire controlled the part of the world where the Christian movement began.

Rome ruled by careful organization and by acquiring information about its subjects. Thus Emperor Caesar Augustus demanded that a census for purposes of taxation be taken of all the people within the empire. Each person was required to return to the place of birth to be registered. In compliance with this edict Mary and Joseph journeyed to Bethlehem. There Jesus was born (Luke 2:1–20).

The Roman Empire sometimes delegated authority to local rulers, such as Herod, who was ruler or king of the territory in which Jesus was born. When the Wise Men told Herod they had journeyed to see the newborn king, Herod feared this child would be a threat to his throne. Therefore he ordered the death of all infants and children two years old and younger who lived in Bethlehem (Matthew 2:1–18). Jesus escaped, his parents having been warned in a dream by an angel to flee.

Thus, the very beginning of the Christian movement was accompanied by persecution. Persecution has continued to be a threat to the Christian movement in one form or another ever since.

Jesus' earthly ministry emphasized the importance of religious freedom. He proclaimed that he had come to set people free (Luke 4:16–21). The Jewish people lived under strict rules and regulations developed and enforced by religious authorities. Jesus realized that much of this ritual robbed people of the joyful, free worship of God that was the right of every person. By his teachings and actions Jesus endeavored to set people free (John 8:31–32).

In his ministry, Jesus consistently followed the principles of religious freedom. He never coerced anyone to become his disciple. Jesus indicated that people were free to believe or not to believe in him, but they were held accountable for their choice (John 3:16–21). Some believed and followed him, but some did not (Matt. 19:16–22).

Jesus spoke harshly of the religious leaders and their depriving people of freedom. He promised to set people free. In so doing he ignited the anger of the Jewish religious leaders (John 8:33–59). They in turn aroused resistance among the people to Jesus, claiming he was a heretic. As a result, Jesus encountered increasing hostility during his brief three-year earthly ministry. The religious leaders succeeded in getting Jesus arrested and charged with heresy. He was tried before the Sanhedrin, the religious supreme court of the Jews (Luke 22:66–71).

Rome delegated a great deal of authority to the Sanhedrin, but not that of the death penalty. The authority to impose the death penalty was reserved for Roman governors. Therefore, the religious leaders developed the false accusation against Jesus that he opposed payment of taxes to Caesar, claimed to be a king, and was a threat to Roman authority. This was a criminal charge, not a religious one.

Although Roman authorities were tolerant of various religions, they were highly intolerant of any threat to order. Too, they were vicious in putting down any danger to the rule of Rome. Pontius Pilate, the Roman governor, reluctantly agreed to the execution of Jesus by crucifixion. Although Pilate said he found no basis for the charges against Jesus, he gave in to the pressure of the mob calling for Jesus' crucifixion (Luke 23:1–25).

Thus the religious and civil authorities collaborated in the persecution and death of Jesus. This sinister combination was a harbinger of things to come. The union of religion and government would result in the mutilation and death of multitudes of Christians in the centuries that followed.

Persecution Under the Roman Empire

At first only the Jewish religious authorities and not the Romans were involved in the persecution of the Christians. Rome initially considered the Christian movement as a sect of Judaism, and Judaism was an officially tolerated religion.

Persecution by Jewish Religious Leaders

After Jesus' resurrection, the proclamation of the gospel by Jesus' disciples through the power of the Holy Spirit resulted in thousands of people coming to faith in Christ. The apostles clearly believed in freedom of choice. For example, in Peter's sermon at Pentecost he declared, "Repent and be baptized" (Acts 2:38). The huge response of the people stirred the Jewish religious leaders to try to stifle the Christian movement (Acts 1—8).

The temple authorities in Jerusalem had armed police at their disposal. Unwilling to grant the new movement religious freedom, they ordered the police to arrest the leaders of the Christian movement. The religious authorities threatened them, demanding that they not speak about Jesus. The apostles replied that they must obey God, not human beings (Acts 4:19–20; 5:29). Thus what was to continue for centuries began in the first century: the denial of religious liberty and persecution of Christians by religious authorities.

This persecution became increasingly severe. Stephen, a leader in the Jerusalem church, was stoned to death for his testimony about Jesus (Acts 6:8—7:60). His death was an example of an act of cruel execution by religious leaders on someone who held beliefs different from their own. Such atrocities were repeated tens of thousands of times in the following years.

So severe was the persecution that most of the followers of Christ were driven out of Jerusalem. As they traveled, they shared Christ. Thus the gospel spread, partly as a result of persecution. One of the early persecutors, Saul, became a follower of Christ and, known generally as Paul, helped to spread the gospel through his preaching, teaching, and writing (Acts 9:1-30).

Persecution by Roman Authorities

The ministry of Paul brought the Roman government once again into collaboration with the religious authorities. Several times during his traveling ministry Paul encountered opposition from the Jewish religious leaders or from people who worshiped one or more of the various pagan gods. When the opposition turned into a riot, the Roman officials became involved (Acts 19:1-41). The Romans were not tolerant of riots and disorder.

Such a situation was the cause of a long imprisonment of Paul by Roman authorities. While in Jerusalem on a mission of mercy, Paul became the innocent center of a riot at the temple. The Jewish religious leaders accused Paul of being the cause of the riot. Paul was arrested by the Romans, not for his religious views but because he allegedly had created disorder (Acts 22:22—23:35).

Paul was a Roman citizen and demanded to be treated as a citizen, even appealing his case to Caesar (Acts 26:32). The last part of the Book of Acts tells the story of his imprisonment and being taken to Rome as a prisoner (Acts 21—28). Once again religious authorities used the government in efforts to stifle religious freedom and the Christian movement.

A few years later Rome began to persecute Christians apart from any instigation by Jewish religious leaders. The Roman emperors increasingly demanded that people worship pagan gods. Some emperors even claimed they themselves were gods and should be worshiped. Failure to worship them brought severe punishment. Christians would not worship pagan gods or Caesar as Lord. For them, only Jesus was Lord.

The early Christians' commitment to the lordship of Jesus Christ set the example for generations to follow in their insistence on religious freedom. They believed no person other than Jesus is due worship and no one should claim lordship except Jesus.

Since the early Christians would not hail the emperor as Lord or give in to government efforts to force them to do so, these early followers of Christ suffered terrible persecution. Treason was the basic charge against the Christians by the empire because in the Roman mind the state's welfare depended on all people following the religious rituals prescribed by the government.

Under the tyrannical rule of Rome, thousands of Christians were massacred in the first three centuries of the Christian movement. Godly people who were no threat to Rome endured terrible torture and death. An example of this treatment was the elderly Polycarp. Polycarp, a disciple of the Apostle John, was leader of the church at Smyrna.

The account of Polycarp's execution in A.D. 168 indicates the cruelty of Roman persecution and the lack of religious freedom:

> *The Stadholder [governor] admonished him to have compassion for his great age, and, by swearing by the Emperor's fortune, to deny Christ. Thereupon Polycarp gave the following candid reply, "I have now served my Lord Christ Jesus eighty-six years, and He has never done me any harm. How can I deny my King, who hath hitherto preserved me from all evil, and so faithfully redeemed me?"*

After being threatened with wild beasts and fire, Polycarp said, "But why delayest thou? Bring on the beasts, or the fire, or whatever thou mayest choose: thou shalt not, by either of them, move me to deny Christ, my Lord and Saviour."[4]

In times of the most severe persecutions, the fury and cruelty of the Roman state against the Christian movement resulted in torture and forms of execution too horrible to detail. The result of the entanglement of religion and government in the Roman Empire should have sent a warning signal to future generations to avoid such entanglement. Unfortunately, most failed to heed the warning.

A Catastrophic Turn in "The Freedom Road"

Even under the lash of persecution, the Christian movement grew. Some Roman emperors viciously persecuted Christians, but some did not. When Constantine became emperor, the entire situation changed. Some thought it was for the better, but ultimately it proved for the worse.

The Influence of Constantine

Throughout the first three centuries of the Christian movement, the Roman Empire experienced numerous murders, battles, and intrigues as people vied to rule the empire. In A.D. 312 Constantine defeated a rival for control of the western part of the empire. Of the decisive battle, the historian Williston Walker states,

> But on the eve of the battle at the Mulvian Bridge, Constantine had a dream in which he saw the initial letters of the name of Christ with the words, "By this sign you will conquer." Taking this as an omen, he resolved to trust his cause to the God of the Christians and had the Chi-Rho monogram painted on the shields of his soldiers.[5]

Constantine won the battle and thereafter favored the Christian religion.

In A.D. 313 Constantine and Licinius, the ruler of the eastern part of the empire, issued the Edict of Milan. The edict legitimized Christianity and was intended to bring a halt to persecution of Christians. However, Licinius reneged on the promise and began persecution. Constantine attacked and defeated him in A.D. 324. Constantine thereafter halted persecution of Christians. Williston Walker comments, "Constantine was the sole ruler of the empire, and churches awoke to find that the cause of Rome and the cause of Christ had become one."[6]

Constantine did not make Christianity the official religion of the empire, but he favored Christianity and provided many benefits. He was not baptized until shortly before his death and continued through his reign to patronize various gods. However, when he built a new city, often termed the "New Rome," he filled it with Christian churches and symbols, not pagan idols and temples. It became known as Constantinople (now Istanbul).

Constantine wielded great influence on the development of the Christian movement. Historian Robert Baker notes,

> *Although Christianity did not become the official religion of the Roman Empire until the closing years of the fourth century, the work of the Emperor Constantine (A.D. 323–337) in controlling church life and showering favors upon Christians began the melancholy story of union between the secular and religious leadership that has cursed the world from that time to the present.[7]*

One of the disastrous consequences of church-state union was the stream of people who came into the churches after the government favored Christianity. Prior to this time only convinced believers were in the churches. Historian Bruce Shelley states,

> *Now many came who were politically ambitious, religiously disinterested, and still half-rooted in paganism. This threatened to produce not only shallowness and permeation by pagan superstitions but also the secularization and misuse of religion for political purposes.[8]*

In A.D. 325 Constantine called all of the bishops in the empire to meet at Nicaea to settle certain theological disputes. Constantine presided, an ominous sign of the beginning of the union of church and state. It would not be the last time that a government official utilized church leaders to expand and consolidate power.

The Union of Church and State

In A.D. 380 a major step toward church-state union took place. The
Roman rulers Gratian and Theodosius I "made belief in Christianity a matter of imperial command."[9] Williston Walker comments,
"Clearly, in the minds of Gratian and Theodosius, Christianity was
now the official religion of the empire, and all others were forbidden, including deviant forms of Christianity itself."[10] The command
did not bring religious freedom but rather intensified persecution
of those who did not agree with the doctrines of the official government-supported church.

The Roman belief that the welfare of the empire depended on religion led to the establishment of Christianity as the official religion
because the emperors concluded that Christianity (their version) was
the best religion for the sake of the empire. Therefore, people who
did not believe and worship in accord with the official religion were
considered traitors and worthy of death.

The imperial decree stated:

> *It is Our Will that all the peoples we rule shall practice that religion
> which the divine Peter the Apostle transmitted to the Romans. We shall
> believe in the single Deity of the Father, the Son, and the Holy Spirit,
> under the concept of equal majesty and of the Holy Trinity.*
>
> *We command that those persons who follow this rule shall embrace
> the name of Catholic Christians. The rest, however, whom We adjudge
> demented and insane, shall sustain the infamy of heretical dogmas,
> their meeting places shall not receive the name of churches, and they
> shall be smitten first by divine vengeance and secondly by the retribu-
> tion of Our own initiative, which We shall assume in accordance with
> divine judgment.*[11]

The emperors lavished financial support and positions of power
on leaders of the official church. Too, they continued to influence the
development of what they considered to be orthodoxy by punishing
those they deemed unorthodox. Their primary motive was to have a
strong unified state. They believed that a strong nation depended on

a common religion enforced by the government and held by all citizens. This view later held sway in what was termed *Christendom.*

Due to various causes the churches of the western and eastern portions of the empire drifted apart and developed different approaches to theology, worship, and organization. Rome became the dominant center of the western portion and Constantinople that of the eastern. From this point on in our journey on "the freedom road," we will focus on the West, for in the West religious freedom as we know it finally emerged—but only after a long and bloody struggle.

The Relation of Church and State

As the Roman Empire crumbled, weakened by corruption from within and attacks from without, the leaders of the Roman Catholic Church grew more and more powerful. The bishop of Rome became the head of the type of Christian movement that had the favor of the government. The development of the papacy was well under way. By the mid A.D. 400s, the bishop of Rome had become the authoritarian head of the churches in the West, a position affirmed by the emperor.

The doctrines of the Roman Catholic Church likewise were being developed and enforced. For example, salvation from hell to heaven was only through the sacraments administered by the church. Infants received baptism, one of the sacraments. Sprinkling or pouring of water began to replace immersion as the form of baptism. The Lord's Supper became a ceremony in which the bread and juice were transformed into the body and blood of Christ by the words of a priest. The Latin translation of the Bible by Jerome, the Vulgate, became the "normative version of the Scriptures for churches in communion with the see of Rome."[12] Any who did not follow the teachings of the church could be excommunicated, cutting them off from the sacraments,

Throughout most of the Middle Ages[13] in Europe a constant struggle existed between the pope and the political leaders for supremacy. First one and then the other claimed ultimate authority. Pope Leo III crowned Charlemagne as emperor in A.D. 800.

Such an act might indicate the supremacy of church over state, but not so. "As emperor, Charlemagne felt called to rule his people both in civil and in ecclesiastical matters. He appointed bishops just as he named generals...."[14] He also forced people whom he conquered to be baptized.

Later popes attempted to assure the supremacy of church over state. In the latter part of the eleventh century Pope Gregory VII in the *Dictatus Papae* (Dictates of the Pope) issued a collection of brief statements that summarized official views of the Roman Catholic Church. Included were these statements about the pope:

"That he alone can depose or reinstate bishops."
"That he alone may use imperial insignia."
"That he himself may be judged of no one."
"That he may absolve subjects from their fealty to wicked men."[15]

This edict in essence declared that in the union of church and state the church was the superior partner. In a showdown between the pope and kings, King Henry IV resisted papal authority and as a result was excommunicated. Never before had a pope deposed a king. In A.D. 1077 the king humbled himself in the snow for three days outside a castle at Canossa, where the pope was residing. Only then did Pope Gregory VII release him from excommunication.

Persecutions by Church and State

For the next few centuries regardless of whether church or state seemed to be in ultimate control, the official governments for the most part carried out the basic wishes of the Roman Catholic Church. The Roman Catholic faith was enforced by government officials. Religious freedom did not exist.

Not everyone followed the dictates of the Roman Catholic Church, however. History records that various groups maintained their own beliefs and worship practices that were contrary to the official ones. Likely there were others not recorded in history. These various groups endeavored to exercise religious freedom by practicing their own faith, but they were severely persecuted by the official church and the government in power. People labeled as "heretics" were hounded, arrested, humiliated, beaten, tortured, and often executed. Threatened with death if they did not confess belief in the "official" doctrines of the state-supported church, many refused and were burned alive.

The Waldensians are an example of such a group. The founder of the movement was Waldes (about A.D. 1140–1218), a wealthy merchant of Lyons. In what he considered obedience to the teaching of Christ, he gave up his wealth and committed himself to living in poverty and preaching in public. He believed "the Bible, especially the New Testament, is the sole rule of belief and life."[16] The Roman Catholic Church responded by excommunicating his followers, known as the Waldensians. Other groups that refused to abide by the official rule of the Roman Catholic Church were also excommunicated and condemned as heretics.

However, various "heretical" groups continued to grow, exercising what they considered a right to practice their faith freely and preach publicly. In an effort to stamp out such groups, the Roman Catholic Church established the papal Inquisition or Holy Office in A.D. 1233. It "developed into a most formidable and fearsome organ."[17] Using heinous torture to root out heretics and secure confessions, the church inquisitors turned condemned people over to civil magistrates for punishment. Those so condemned usually suffered the penalty of being burned alive at the stake in a public ceremony.

Church and state, pope and emperor, often were divided in a struggle for ultimate authority. However, they were united in efforts to crush religious freedom. Various Scriptures were interpreted to justify harsh persecution, even death, such as Luke 14:15–24.[18] In the minds of both civic and church leaders, religious freedom was a threat not only to the souls of people but also to the stability of society. To allow "heretics" freedom to share their views was considered irresponsible. To undermine the authority of the established church was to threaten the concept of the divine right of kings and therefore the stability of government.

Thus those who were considered to be heretics were viewed as a threat not only to the Roman Catholic Church but also to kings. Those who would not bow to the union of church and state were considered not only to be heretics but also traitors. The general population believed such people deserved to be exterminated, much as a dreaded disease needed to be eradicated.

Uniformity in doctrine, not diversity, was considered a model society, even if such uniformity had to be gained by force. The pattern of the New Testament churches was abandoned. The example of Jesus in always using persuasion and never coercion was ignored. The spirit of the Jewish Sanhedrin and of the pagan Roman emperors who abhorred religious freedom prevailed.

Conclusion

In the midst of the Middle Ages, any hope of religious freedom seemed ridiculous. The forces of an established church and the power of secular rulers welded together appeared to be an impregnable defense against any effort for religious freedom. However, just when such freedom seemed impossible, the first glimmers of a new day began to be evident. That is the subject of the next chapters.

> *"Peter and the other apostles replied: 'We must obey God rather than men!'"*
>
> ACTS 5:29

CHAPTER *Two*

The Beginning of the Struggle for Religious Freedom

"Government has no more to do with the religious opinions of men, than it has with the principles of mathematics."

—JOHN LELAND[1]
(1754–1841) Baptist preacher,
Advocate for church-state separation

ONLY BY BEING AWARE OF the past can we truly appreciate the freedom we enjoy in the present. From the time of Christ until the 1600s people knew no religious freedom and little religious toleration. During most of this period, anyone who dared express religious views contrary to the official ones of the prevailing government and/ or the official church did so at peril of life.

Walking "the freedom road" took courage born out of deep convictions based on the teachings of the Bible. The future of religious freedom looked bleak indeed, but developments were beginning to take place that would give some hope. For freedom to emerge, the dominance of the Roman Catholic Church and later of the Protestant religious movements that were allied with governments had to be broken. Over several centuries that is what finally happened, but only after the blood of those who suffered and died for religious freedom had poured into the soil and rivers of Europe.

Changes That Laid the Groundwork for Freedom

Major changes occurred during the period in Europe from the 700s through the 1500s that would finally have a positive effect on freedom. Some of these were economic and political. Others were cultural and intellectual. All of them together, directly or indirectly, paved the way for religious freedom.

The Influence of the Crusades

Ironically, a movement that at first brought further restrictions on freedom—Islam—ultimately, although indirectly, brought about changes that aided the development of religious liberty. In the A.D. 600s, Muhammad launched a new religion and united a huge part of the Arab people around its teachings. Islam was spread by the sword. The Moslem armies swept across huge territories that had once been dominated by Christians, including Jerusalem and the Holy Land.

Moslems tolerated Jews and Christians to some degree as *people of the Book* since all three religions have roots in the Old Testament. However, Jews and Christians were allowed no real freedom of religion. Efforts to convert Moslems to being Christians carried the penalty of death and "Moslem law made death the penalty for unrepentant apostasy from Islam."[2]

The spread of Islam into western Europe came to a halt at the Battle of Tours in A.D. 732, but the Holy Land remained in Moslem control. Christians from Europe made pilgrimages to the Holy Land and for years were allowed to do so. However, pilgrims began to report that they were being persecuted by Moslems.

In A.D. 1095 Pope Urban II called for crusades against the Moslems to retake Jerusalem. As a result of early victories, the crusaders gained control of the Holy Land. Then as Islamic forces prevailed, the Holy Land reverted to Moslem control.[3] Various crusades occurred over the next 400 years but with little success. Today we still encounter the hostility of many Moslems over the slaughter of the Islamic people by the crusaders.

The crusaders returning from the East brought with them knowledge that had been practically lost in the West for centuries, including the teachings of Greek philosophers, such as Aristotle. Historian William R. Estep observes, "As a result, life and learning in medieval Europe would never again be quite the same."[4] Centuries would pass before the impact of the knowledge brought back by the crusaders had much effect on "the freedom road." However, ultimately it helped lay the foundation for the Renaissance with its emphasis on freedom of inquiry.

Economic, Political, and Social Changes

During most of what is termed the Middle Ages the basis of wealth had been land, with agriculture dominating the economy. For various reasons the economy of Europe began to move more toward trade and commerce. New groups of influential people developed, such as merchants and bankers. Cities grew because centers were needed for trade and banking.

Merchants and bankers began to challenge the supremacy of nobles and feudal landowners. Kings tended to strengthen their own centralized power by siding with the merchants and bankers. One result of this was the development of countries with a sense of nationalism. The historian Justo Gonzáles noted, "Nationalism in turn undermined the papal claims to universal authority."[5]

Cultural and Intellectual Changes

Events at the turn of the sixteenth century literally opened up new worlds. The "discovery" of America in 1492, the extensive exploration of the world that followed, the expansion of trade, and the availability of printed materials all contributed to massive changes.

The cultural and intellectual changes are usually referred to as the Renaissance. These changes were complex and are difficult to define. However, in regard to religious freedom, perhaps their main contribution was an emphasis on the worth of the individual person and on human achievement and ability. One aspect of the Renaissance focused on literature and ways of thinking about human life. The influx of ancient Greek classical literature, brought about in part by the Crusades, made a profound impact on scholars. One such scholar was Desiderius Erasmus (about A.D. 1466–1536).[6]

Although Erasmus freely criticized the Roman Catholic Church, he did not want to break with it. He wanted to reform the church, which had become increasingly materialistic and corrupt, by teaching and writing to bring about a return to the Bible, the church fathers, and the ancient Greek writers.

One of Erasmus's methods of reform was to publish a Greek New Testament, accompanied by a Latin translation and critical notes. The invention of moveable-type printing by Johann Gutenberg in the mid 1400s made possible mass production of written materials. As a result the Bible was printed in numerous languages, including the Greek New Testament by Erasmus.

Thus the Bible became available to people who were able to read the Bible for themselves. Prior to this time, copies of the Bible were made laboriously by hand, and few were available. With Bibles in hand, people were able to compare the teaching of the Bible with the teaching and practices of the Roman Catholic Church and determine for themselves what true Christianity was. This capability paved the way for the Reformation.

Challenges to Roman Catholic Religious Monopoly

For religious freedom to emerge, the government-enforced religious monopoly of the Roman Catholic Church had to be eliminated. Although many factors led to this development, the challenges to this authority made by people who were either priests or members of the Roman Catholic Church played a major role.

Early Challengers to the Roman Catholic Church

One of the first indications of a possible break in the power of the Roman Catholic Church came with the life and teachings of John Wycliffe (about A.D. 1329–1384), an English priest and educator. He advocated that the Bible was the only authority for faith and practice, not the pope or the traditions of the church.

Wycliffe also insisted that the Bible should be available to all people. He and his followers translated the Bible into English so that it could be read and studied by the laity. He taught that the church was not composed of the pope and clergy alone, which was the teaching of the official church, but of all of the redeemed. He did not oppose the union of church and state but tended to elevate the power of the king over that of the pope.

Itinerant preachers called Lollards spread Wycliffe's views. His views caused him to be excommunicated from the Roman Catholic Church. After his death, his writings were banned and burned by the church and his bones dug from the grave and burned.

But the church could not quench the light of reform Wycliffe had ignited. John Huss (about A.D. 1369–1415), a Czech Roman Catholic priest, accepted many of Wycliffe's teachings. Huss emphasized that Jesus Christ, not the pope, was the head of the church and the supreme judge of humankind.

For Huss, only the Bible was authoritative. Huss was clearly sounding one of the chords in what was to become the Baptist symphony of freedom. Because of his views on the authority of the Bible and the teachings of the Bible, the Roman Catholic Church threatened Huss, excommunicated him, and finally arrested him. He was tried for heresy, condemned, and burned at the stake. The church-state union responded to challenges with harsh persecution. Huss was one of thousands who perished as the iron-fisted control of Europe by the collaboration of the church and the government began to be tested by people who challenged certain teachings of the church.

The Reformation and Lack of Religious Freedom

The Reformation brought the greatest challenge to the dominance of the Roman Catholic Church, but it did not directly bring an increase of religious freedom. People such as Wycliffe and Huss made many of the basic emphases of the Reformation, but no large-scale movement took place until the Reformation.

Martin Luther (A.D. 1483–1546), a Roman Catholic monk and theologian who lived in Germany, is usually credited with initiating the Reformation. On October 31, 1517, he courageously posted ninety-five theses on the door of the Castle Church in Wittenberg. These statements not only protested corruption in the Roman Catholic Church but also challenged certain teachings of the church. A lengthy debate ensued between Luther and his followers and that of the officials representing the pope.

Luther's teachings are voluminous, but two emphases were primary: (1) The Bible is the sole authority for faith and practice, not the traditions and teachings of the pope and the Roman Catholic Church. (2) Salvation comes only by faith in Christ, not by sacraments or good works.

Luther was condemned as a heretic. At his trial Roman Catholic Church leaders demanded him to recant. His reply was that if he could be shown to be in error by the teachings of the Bible he would recant, but otherwise he could not. His reply is famous: "Here I stand. I can do no other."

Tension had existed for many years between the German princes and the popes. Thus for various reasons many of the German political leaders sided with Luther and gave him protection from the pope. Luther launched a new denomination, the Lutheran Church. It was supported by the governments in most areas of northern Europe. Therefore, union of church and state continued, and religious freedom did not develop.

John Calvin (A.D. 1509–1564), another leader in the Reformation, advocated views similar to Luther's but in some ways significantly different. A brilliant scholar, he developed what is termed *reformed theology*, which he set forth in *The Institutes of Religion*. Calvin spent most of his ministry in Geneva, Switzerland. He advocated that the magistrate, that is, the government leaders, had responsibility to uphold the true faith—the faith *he* taught. Those who disagreed could be charged with heresy. Calvin taught that the government had a responsibility to punish them, even with death.

A well-known person put to death in Geneva for heresy was Michael Servetus. He was burned at the stake in Geneva by the civil authorities in A.D. 1553. Thus many people remember Calvin "primarily as 'the man who burned Servetus.'"[7] Clearly "the freedom road" did not run through Geneva. Church and state collaborated to preserve a particular brand of Christianity.

Ulrich Zwingli (A.D. 1484–1531), another leader in the Protestant Reformation, taught and preached in Zurich, Switzerland. Religious freedom did not exist here, but a movement that would contribute greatly to freedom did come to the fore here, the Anabaptists. Zwingli, a Roman Catholic priest, became a careful student of the New Testament, including the Greek translation Erasmus had produced. His studies led him to challenge many of the traditional teachings and practices of the Roman Catholic Church. In alliance with the city council of Zurich, he preached and taught reform, but he did not advocate freedom of religion.

King Henry VIII of England (A.D. 1491–1547) led a break with the Roman Catholic Church in that country. In 1534 he declared the Church of England to be independent and named himself as head of the Church of England. In a sense, the tightest union of church and state occurred in England, with the head of the government also being the head of the established church. King Henry VIII and his successors did not believe in religious freedom and dealt harshly with dissenters, including Baptists, as we shall see in the next chapter.

The use of the power of the state to carry out the religious convictions of the Protestant Reformers led to catastrophic results for freedom of religion. Religious groups, however, seem slow to learn from history. The historian Estep observes that

some modern evangelicals seem quite willing to abandon the "freedom with which Christ has set us free" for some form of religious

establishment in an attempt to counteract the forces of disintegration
that threaten to destroy contemporary society. It is apparently always
a temptation, when the wellsprings of spiritual vitality begin to run
dry, to resort to the arm of flesh to fight the battles of the Lord. The
history of the Reformation should teach us that this is a temptation
that can only end in dashed hopes.[8]

The Anabaptist Pioneers for Religious Freedom

The reformations led by Luther, Calvin, Zwingli, and Henry VIII
enjoyed the support of government power in enforcing their views.
These reformations did not include religious freedom. However,
another aspect of the Protestant Reformation did stress religious
freedom and separation of church and state. Often termed the
Radical Reformation, it was led by people labeled *Anabaptists*. Their
enemies gave them this name because of their insistence on baptism
for believers only, thus appearing to re-baptize people who had been
"baptized" as infants.[9] (The prefix *ana* means *again*.)

Protestant Persecution of Early Anabaptists

The beginning of the Anabaptist movement is usually traced to
Zurich, although certain Anabaptist beliefs can be traced from
New Testament times. Zwingli, the leader of the reform movement
in Zurich, used his knowledge of Greek and the classics to attract
young humanist scholars to study with him, including studying the
Greek New Testament. By the fall of A.D. 1521, Conrad Grebel (about
1498–1526), a young vagabond scholar, joined Zwingli's study group.
A year later Grebel had also become eager for reform, but his convictions took him beyond those of his teacher.

   In January of 1525 Grebel and a small group of his allies entered
a public dispute with Zwingli. They argued that infant baptism was
wrong. They lost the argument. Since Zwingli had the backing of the city
council, Grebel and his followers had three choices: conform to Zwingli's
views; leave Zurich; or face imprisonment. They chose the latter.

In late January of 1525 approximately a dozen men of Grebel's persuasion met in the house of Felix Manz (about 1498–1527, sometimes spelled *Mantz*), one of the group who had studied with Zwingli. After much prayer George Blaurock (about 1491–1529), another of Zwingli's students, asked Conrad Grebel to baptize him. Blaurock knelt down, and Grebel baptized him by pouring water over his head. Then Blaurock baptized all of the others who were in the house.[10] The group pledged to live lives pleasing to Christ and to teach the gospel to others.

William Estep, a scholar of the Anabaptist movement, states,

This was clearly the most revolutionary act of the Reformation. No other event so completely symbolized the break with Rome. Here, for the first time in the course of the Reformation, a group of Christians dared to form a church after what was conceived to be the New Testament pattern.[11]

True to their commitment to teach the gospel to others, Grebel and Manz went from house to house witnessing, baptizing, and conducting the Lord's Supper. Among those baptized was Wolfgang Ulimann, a former monk. Ulimann requested Grebel to baptize him, not by pouring, but by immersion. Grebel complied and dipped him completely under the waters of the Rhine River. Ulimann became a zealous advocate of the gospel and of believer's baptism.

The Anabaptist movement grew rapidly. Hundreds of adults were baptized. Zwingli and the government officials responded by arresting Grebel, Blaurock, and Manz. Many false charges were brought against them, but the accusation that they taught and practiced believer's baptism as the sign of membership in the true church was accurate. They insisted that since this is what the Bible taught, they must obey the Bible. Many other Anabaptists were arrested and imprisoned. Their prayers and singing filled the prison tower.

A new law in Zurich made the act of performing baptism of adults a crime punishable by death. Grebel and others escaped prison. Grebel ministered only a short time before dying of the plague in 1526. Manz continued to teach and to baptize—and to be arrested. As Estep states,

"Hardly a prison in the vicinity of Manz's labors escaped being honored by his presence."[12] In January of 1527 he was sentenced to death.

Manz, bound by the wrists, was taken from prison to the Limmat River. Along the way he preached to the crowd, praising God and declaring that believer's baptism was the true baptism according to the word of God and the teachings of Christ. His mother's voice could be heard urging him to remain faithful. George H. Williams in *The Radical Reformation* describes Manz's execution:

> *He was trussed, with a stick thrust between his roped, doubled-up legs and arms, and as he was being drawn into the icy water he sang, "In manus tuas domine commendo spiritum meum" [Into thy hands, O Lord, I commend my spirit.].*[13]

Manz's execution by drowning was the first martyrdom of an Anabaptist at the hands of a Protestant government. Many other Anabaptist deaths would follow. For example, Blaurock continued to spread the Anabaptist beliefs. Frequently arrested, on one occasion he was beaten so badly that his blood ran through the street. Ultimately he was condemned and burned at the stake on September 6, 1529. But neither death by fire nor by water could halt the Anabaptist movement in the area where the Swiss Reformation was taking place.

Roman Catholic Persecution of Anabaptists

Roman Catholics also hounded, imprisoned, and executed Anabaptists. No religious freedom existed in the territories dominated by the Roman Catholic Church.

One horrible example of this persecution was the death of Michael Sattler (about A.D. 1495–1527), an Anabaptist leader. Sattler was arrested in Rottenburg, which was under Austrian authority. The king of Austria was Roman Catholic and ordered Sattler's execution. Sattler's executioners first tortured him by tearing out a part of his tongue and then twice ripping pieces of his body with red-hot tongs. Sattler was placed in a cart, and on the way to the place of his death his flesh was torn five more times by the tongs. Sattler prayed for his persecutors before being tied to a ladder and pushed into the flames. When the fire burned through the ropes that tied his hands, he lifted two forefingers as a signal that a martyr's death was bearable. Then from his seared lips and torn tongue came the words, "Father, I commend my spirit unto Thy hands." Sattler's wife was drowned eight days later, one among a multitude of Anabaptist women who suffered death for their faith.[14]

Balthasar Hubmaier (about A.D. 1480–1528) was perhaps the most influential Anabaptist to suffer at the hands of the Roman Catholic Church. He is especially important in the story of religious freedom, for he argued brilliantly for religious liberty and against any effort to force people to embrace any particular religion.

Hubmaier served as a priest in Waldshut. His study of the Bible, especially the Pauline epistles, led him to a conversion experience. In 1525 Wilhelm Reublin, who had been driven from Zurich by Zwingli because of his beliefs on baptism, baptized Hubmaier and sixty others. On Easter, Hubmaier then baptized more than 300 people and later conducted the Lord's Supper in a simple, non-sacramental style, far different from the Roman Catholic Mass.

Hubmaier considered the Bible to be the sole authority for faith and practice. On the authority of the Bible, he declared that faith in Christ cannot be coerced but must be freely given. He proclaimed that the Bible taught baptism was only for those who had placed their faith in Christ as Lord and Savior voluntarily. Thus he opposed infant baptism. He wrote a pamphlet on religious liberty in which, on the basis of the Bible's teachings, he condemned the burning of heretics.

In his writings Hubmaier set forth several basic beliefs that are foundational for religious freedom. He insisted that the Bible is the sole authority for the Christian life and church, giving special emphasis to the New Testament. He championed free will, believing it a necessary basis for moral responsibility. Of this view Estep wrote, "Neither the sovereignty of God nor the grace of God nullified for Hubmaier the necessity of an uncoerced response to the gospel."[15] Thus people should be free to preach the gospel and free to respond, be baptized, and become part of a church of their choice.

Some Anabaptists (for there were several varieties of Anabaptists) were pacifists and believed that a magistrate could not be a Christian. Hubmaier disagreed. He argued that the Bible sets forth the legitimacy of government and of Christians serving in government positions. Hubmaier believed that the use of the sword by governments could be justified but never to coerce religious belief. In regard to unjust governments, Hubmaier implied that armed insurrection is forbidden a Christian.

Hubmaier, persecuted both by Roman Catholics and Protestants, found refuge in Moravia, a tolerant city. Moravia, though, fell under control of the Roman Catholic king of Austria, Ferdinand I. He had Hubmaier and his wife imprisoned. Hubmaier suffered the torture of the rack, but he did not recant. On March 10, 1528, he was executed. In *The Radical Reformation*, George Williams describes his death:

> *As his clothes were stripped from him, he . . . repeated in Latin the words of Jesus: "In manus tuas, Domine, commendo spiritum meum." [Into thy hands, O Lord, I commend my spirit.] When sulphur and gunpowder were rubbed into his hair and long beard, he imploringly cried: "Oh, salt me well, salt me well!" As they took flame, his last word was . . . "O Jesus, Jesus."*[16]

A few days later his wife was thrown into the Danube River with a large stone tied around her neck.[17]

Menno Simons and Religious Freedom

Anabaptists spread across Europe, dogged by persecution everywhere they went. Lutherans, Roman Catholics, and followers of the Reformed tradition all attempted to eradicate the various expressions of Anabaptist belief and practice.

When Anabaptists reached the Netherlands, one of the most significant leaders joined the movement: Menno Simons (A.D. 1496–1561). Of him Estep writes, "There is no greater name among Anabaptists of the sixteenth century than that of Menno Simons."[18]

Menno was ordained a priest in the Catholic Church in 1524 at the age of twenty-eight. The contents of the Bible were unknown to him at the time. He came to question that the bread and wine of the Mass were the flesh and blood of Christ as the Roman Catholic Church taught. His questioning led him to study the New Testament. This study caused him to doubt both transubstantiation and infant baptism. However, he remained a priest with a worldly lifestyle.

In 1535 he learned that 300 Anabaptists had been put to death at the Old Cloister, where they had sought refuge from persecution. Among them was his brother. Menno had come to appreciate the quality of life of the Anabaptists. He contrasted their purity with his worldliness. After a time of agonizing soul-searching, Menno placed his faith in Christ as Lord and Savior. Soon he accepted Anabaptist views, left the priesthood, and joined the Anabaptist movement. He did this at considerable sacrifice, for he left security of position to identify with a group despised by Protestants and Roman Catholics alike.

Menno Simons was such an acknowledged leader among the Anabaptists that they became known as Mennonites. The basis of his theological views was the Bible as interpreted through Christ. The Bible was the sole authority for matters of doctrine and discipline. He avoided making any creed-like documents. Apparently he was concerned that a creed might be thought of as superior to the Bible itself or become a test of faith among the Anabaptists. Freedom to develop one's own beliefs according to the Bible was central in his thought.

He insisted that faith alone made a person holy before God and that faith was manifest in works of brotherly love. Baptism was a testimony to saving faith, which was always voluntary. Infant baptism, therefore, was viewed as unbiblical. Baptism was an act of obedience to the command of Christ on the part of a true believer and had no saving significance. However, baptism was nonetheless vitally important in the life of the individual believer and the church.

Simons developed one of the most extensive treatments of the nature of the church by Anabaptists. He indicated that there were two meanings for the word *church* in the New Testament, one for the universal church made up of all of the redeemed and the other for the local fellowship that gathers for teaching, baptism, and the Lord's

Supper under the leadership of a shepherd. The Anabaptists emphasized that a church is a voluntary fellowship of regenerate people. Religious freedom, therefore, was a key to having truly New Testament churches composed of the redeemed.

On the basis of the Bible, Anabaptists insisted that the church and the state were instituted by God but for different purposes and that each should carry out its purpose. The purpose of the state was not to enforce religious views but rather to provide order for society.

Conclusion

In the 1600s and 1700s, Baptists and Anabaptists were often viewed as one movement by rulers and the general population. Baptists endeavored to clarify that the Baptist movement was not the same as the Anabaptist movement. Although Baptists agreed with many Anabaptist teachings, they disagreed with others and did not want to be identified with them. For example, the title page of the London Confession of Baptists in 1644 begins with these words: "The Confession of Faith, Of those Churches which are commonly (though falsely) called Anabaptists."[19]

Furthermore, Baptists did not want to be labeled as Anabaptists because the *Ana* in the term meant *again*. In other words, Anabaptists were viewed as a religious movement that baptized people *again*, that is, after they had first been baptized as infants. Baptists insisted that infant baptism was really no baptism. Therefore, they were not rebaptizing people who made professions of faith in Christ and sought to be baptized. Rather, they were baptizing them for the first time.

Most historians agree that the Anabaptists were the first in the modern era to advocate religious freedom achieved through the separation of church and state. Thus they paved the way for a major widening of "the freedom road" by Baptists and others. That is the story of the next chapter.

CHAPTER *Three*

The Role of Baptists in Bringing Religious Freedom

"Let them be heretics, Turks, Jews, or whatsoever,
it appertains not to the earthly power to
punish them in the least measure."

— THOMAS HELWYS[1]
(1550?–1616?) English Baptist
pastor, Martyr for religious freedom

APTISTS CAN CLAIM NO GREATER contribution than that of their
support of religious liberty, not only for themselves, but for all
persons,"[2] concludes historian Bill Leonard. Baptists have advocated
religious freedom for all people—not freedom for some or toleration
for many, but complete religious liberty for all.

The possibility of religious freedom began to emerge in the 1600s
and took full form in the United States in the late 1700s and early
1800s. No single development or person enabled religious freedom to
come to fruition at this period in history. Instead a series of developments and various people and groups made possible what we enjoy
today. The preceding chapter traces some of those developments that
provided the groundwork for religious liberty.

In the 1600s and 1700s what is usually termed the Enlighten-ment developed from the foundation laid by the Renaissance. John Locke (1632–1704), one of the Enlightenment philosophers, taught that every person had certain natural rights, including the right of liberty. Neither church nor state ought to interfere with the pursuit of these rights.

Baptists agreed that religious liberty ought not be denied by church or state. However, Baptists did not get their belief in religious freedom from politicians or philosophers. The Baptist commitment to religious freedom comes from basic Bible beliefs and an awareness of the horrible history of church-state union.

Nevertheless, Baptists found many people to be allies in their struggle for religious freedom. Historian Hugh Wamble warns that "it is unbecoming braggadocio to claim church-state separation as Baptists' private property."[3]

The Baptist Beginning: Persecution and Testimony

For advocating religious freedom, Baptists endured terrible persecu-tion. Yet circumstances were changing that eventually made religious liberty possible. Let's examine the story of Baptists in helping to build " the freedom road."

Baptists in Amsterdam

The story begins in England. In 1534 King Henry VIII established the Church of England. Various forms of corruption existed in the Church of England. A group of people within the Church endeavored to purify it, to make it conform more to the pattern of the churches in the New Testament. Labeled Puritans, they did not want to break away from the Church of England but desired to purify it from within. Although they did not deny the union of church and state, they nevertheless were persecuted by the Church of England and the government.

Some Puritans came to believe that efforts to correct corrup-tion within the Church of England seemed hopeless. Therefore they separated from the Church of England and became known as Separatists. Government and religious leaders persecuted them severely.

John Smyth (about 1570–1612; sometimes spelled Smith) was one of the pastors of a Separatist group. Educated at Cambridge University and a priest in the Church of England, he was originally part of the Puritan movement. However, along with others, he despaired of purifying the Church and became a Separatist. In order to avoid persecution, he led his little group of followers to Amsterdam in 1609. Amsterdam was one of the few places in Europe where a degree of religious toleration existed.

While in Amsterdam, Smyth carefully studied the Greek New Testament. He insisted that the Bible should be the only authority for the faith and practice of a church. He concluded from his study of the Bible that certain beliefs and practices held by the Separatists, such as infant baptism, were contrary to the New Testament.

Consequently, Smyth baptized himself, believing that his baptism as an infant was not true baptism. He then baptized others in the group that had followed him to Amsterdam, and they constituted a new church. Many historians view this as the first Baptist church of so-called modern times. Smyth declared that church and state should be separate. In his statement of faith concerning religious freedom, he wrote:

> *That the magistrate is not by virtue of his office to meddle with religion, or matters of conscience, to force or compel men to this or that form of religion, or doctrine: but to leave Christian religion free, to every man's conscience, and to handle only civil transgressions (Rom. xiii), injuries and wrongs of man against man, in murder, adultery, theft, etc. for Christ only is the king, and lawgiver of the church and conscience (James iv.12).*[4]

Of this statement historian William Estep declared, *"Smyth's confession of 1612 became the first confession of faith in English to set forth the principles of complete religious liberty and the separation of church and state."*[5]

Baptists in England

Thomas Helwys (about 1550 to about 1615), a member of the Amsterdam congregation, believed that the group should return to England and establish a church according to the New Testament pattern. Smyth disagreed. He wanted to remain in Amsterdam, partly because of his interest in the Mennonite movement that was strong there.

Therefore, Helwys returned to England with a portion of the group from Amsterdam. He established what is considered by many historians to be the first Baptist church on English soil, in Spittlefield, near London.

Helwys believed firmly in religious freedom. In 1612 he wrote a book entitled *A Short Declaration of the Mistery of Iniquity* (often spelled *Mystery* in modern versions), in which he declared that the government had no right to dictate to people what to believe in religious matters or how to organize and govern a church. This book contains one of the earliest and most complete arguments in the English language for the cause of religious freedom.[6]

The Christian commitment and courage of Helwys led him, a poor and politically powerless pastor, to challenge the wealthy and powerful king of England. Helwys sent a copy of his book to King James I with a personal inscription: "The king is a mortall man & not God, therefore hath no power over ye immortal Soules of his Subjects, to make lawes and ordinance for them, and to set Spiritual Lords over them."[7]

The king regarded Helwys as both a heretic and a traitor. He had Helwys thrown in Newgate Prison, a terrible place, filled with rodents, insects, disease, filth—and hardened criminals. Helwys, a devout pastor and peaceful citizen, had done nothing violent or immoral to warrant such punishment.

Helwys had only to agree that the king had the right to dictate belief and practice to Christians and to churches and he would be freed. Yet he would not abandon his convictions. Neither would his wife, Joan Ashmore Helwys, who was also imprisoned. After years of imprisonment Helwys died in Newgate, faithful to the end of his life for the cause of religious freedom.[8]

Puritans and Separatists contended for their religious freedom but not for everyone's. In contrast, Helwys and the other Baptists pled for religious freedom for all. The pleas of Helwys were echoed and elaborated on by a number of Baptists. One of these was John Bunyan (1628–1688), pastor of the Baptist church in Bedford. Bunyan supplemented his income as a pastor by being a tinker, a maker and repairer of pots and pans. Being bi-vocational was common since Baptist congregations were generally small and poor.

Bunyan was arrested in 1660 for holding services not in conformity with those of the Church of England. Locked in jail in January of 1661, he remained imprisoned for twelve years. His first wife, Mary, had been a great influence in his conversion and Christian life but had died leaving John with four children, including a blind daughter. He married his second wife, Elizabeth, in 1659. When he was arrested only a short time afterward, she had the care of the children. She bravely endured great hardship during his confinement and pled with the authorities for his release. They refused, declaring, "His doctrine is the doctrine of the devil."[9]

Bunyan insisted that the gospel should be freely proclaimed and that the government had no right to interfere with that. He was released and then later arrested again for the same cause. While in prison he wrote the English classic, *Pilgrim's Progress*.

Bunyan was one of many Baptist pastors and church members in England who suffered persecution. With the passage of the Act of Toleration in 1689, the worst forms of persecution ceased. However, the Act brought only toleration and not religious freedom.

The Early Baptist Role in Religious Freedom in America

"Religious liberty was born in America," declares historian Glenn Hinson.[10] Religious toleration in various degrees existed, but toleration is not full religious freedom. Baptist theologian Edgar Young Mullins, writing in 1908 about the distinction between religious toleration and freedom, stated, "It is a singular fact, to be noted in this connection, that many writers of great intelligence in other respects even to-day fail to grasp clearly the distinction between religious toleration and religious freedom." He added, "Americans of to-day would no more rest content under a system of mere religious toleration than they were willing to endure taxation without representation under George the Third."[11]

Lack of Religious Freedom

The English colonies in North America provided little or no religious freedom. The first permanent English settlement, Jamestown, was established in 1607 for commercial, not religious reasons. However, religious freedom did not exist in the colony. In 1610 Sir Thomas Gates arrived with the "Laws Divine, Moral and Martial." These laws severely regulated religious observance. For example, those not attending religious services twice daily were subject to whippings and imprisonment.[12] The Church of England became the established official state church in Virginia.

The second colony, that of the Pilgrims at Plymouth in 1620, had a religious basis. Many of those who settled there were Separatists who had suffered persecution in their native England. The persecution caused them to leave England in 1608 and settle in Holland. Later they determined to go to America. They came to the New World for religious freedom, but only for themselves. In fact they established a close connection between church and state that allowed for little or no religious dissent.

However, the Puritans, who arrived ten years later and established the Massachusetts Bay Colony, were even less tolerant. They too came for religious reasons, one of which was to establish a colony ruled by the laws of God as an example to the world. Thus a close relation—in fact, practically a union—of church and state was established. Governor Winthrop of the colony referred to it as "a city upon a hill."[13] Winthrop opposed both democracy, which he described as the "worst of all forms of government," and religious freedom.[14]

Historian Roland Bainton, in *The Travail of Religious Liberty*, described the relationship of church and state in early colonial Massachusetts in this way:

> *Church members alone could vote, and they alone could be church*
> *members who exhibited all the evidences including the emotional signs*
> *of grace. State and Church were one, but Church, State, and community*
> *did not coincide. Those who were not of the Church were not citizens,*
> *but only inhabitants. . . .*[15]

The attitude of those in power in Massachusetts was that if people did not agree with the ruling saints, they could leave. As one Puritan preacher explained the colony's concept of freedom, those who did not agree "have free liberty to keepe away from us."[16] If they chose to stay, the consequences were severe. For example, four Quakers were hanged in the colony.

Some people dared not only to disagree with the Puritan establishment in Massachusetts but also openly to challenge it spiritually and intellectually. One of these was Roger Williams (about 1603–1683), an ordained clergyman of the Puritan persuasion of the Church of England who had been educated at Cambridge. He journeyed with his wife Mary to Massachusetts from England, arriving in Boston in 1631.

Roger Williams developed views of the Christian faith and the relation of church and state that differed radically from those of the ruling establishment of Massachusetts. Williams taught that on the basis of the New Testament, people should be free to worship according to the dictate of conscience, not the dictate of the government. Governments ought not to enforce religious beliefs or practices. Williams also declared that the Indians should be compensated for the land taken from them by the settlers.

These teachings brought on Williams the wrath of the Massachusetts leaders of both church and state. Threatened with forced exile back to England, he fled the colony. He left Mary and their children behind to join him later when he had found a place of safety to settle.

The "Lively Experiment" in Rhode Island

Roger Williams escaped from Massachusetts in the middle of the winter of 1635–36. He likely would have perished in the bitter cold

if the Indians, whom he had defended and befriended, had not provided for and protected him. Traveling south, he purchased land from
the Indians and established the city of Providence and the colony of
Providence Plantations, which later became part of Rhode Island.
There he baptized himself and others, thus "establishing in 1638 the
first church in America of the Baptist (or as the Bay Colony much
preferred to say, Anabaptist) persuasion."[17]

Williams did not remain long as either pastor or Baptist, leaving to become what he termed a Seeker, believing that he had not yet
found the true church. Yet he held fast to his Baptist views, opposing
infant baptism and the union of church and state. In his writings,
such as the *Bloudy Tennent of Persecution for Cause of Conscience* (1644),
he set forth his views of the relation of religion and government. For
example, in the preface he wrote:

> *It is the will and command of* God, *that.* . . . a permission *of the*
> *most* Paganish, Jewish, Turkish, or Anti-christian consciences
> *and* worships, *bee granted to* all *men in all* Nations and Coun-
> tries: *and they are only to be fought against with the* Sword *which*
> *is onely (in* Soule matters*) able to* conquer, *to wit, the* Sword of
> Gods Spirit, *the* Word of God.[18]

Williams called for a strict separation of church and state. He
advocated a "hedge or wall of separation between the Garden of the
Church and the Wilderness of the world."[19] Williams put his views
into action and established a colony that guaranteed complete religious freedom for all. He welcomed Dr. John Clarke (1609–1676), a
physician and preacher, who had left Boston because of his religious
views. Clarke assisted Williams in beginning a settlement. In 1639
Clarke helped found the city of Newport, Rhode Island, and led in
establishing a Baptist church there.[20]

The colony did not have an official charter from the king. Roger
Williams and John Clarke labored for years to secure a charter that
would guarantee full religious freedom. While Clarke was in England
working to secure the charter, Obadiah Holmes (about 1607–1682)
served as pastor of the church in Newport. Clarke wrote *Ill Newes from*

New England in 1652, describing the persecution in New England and setting forth the Baptist views on religious liberty. His scriptural basis against the use of force in religious matters included Jesus' parable of the wheat and weeds in Matthew 13:24–30.[21]

Finally in 1663 Charles II of England granted the charter for the Colony of Rhode Island and Providence Plantations for what was termed "a lively experiment."[22] Thus the historian William Brackney declares that Clarke "brought the first legal sanction to religious liberty in America."[23]

The writings of both Williams and Clarke had a profound influence on Baptists and others in the years following. Leon McBeth declares that "it is certain that Williams helped form the concepts of religious liberty and separation of church and state as held by Baptists in America."[24] The historian Brackney states, "Though Williams is better known, it was John Clarke who, for a longer time and with greater ultimate impact, made the clearest early exposition of the principle of religious freedom for the Baptists."[25]

The Continued Persecution of Baptists in the 1600s

In the meantime, persecution by the established church in New England continued. Baptists and others were discriminated against legally and ostracized socially by the church and the government that supported it.

The severity of the persecution is illustrated by an occurrence in 1651 involving John Clarke, Obadiah Holmes, and John Crandall, a deacon. Clarke gave a personal account of the event in *Ill Newes from New England*, an account that covers many pages. Here is a brief summary of the incident.

The three had traveled from Rhode Island to Massachusetts for a visit. They were arrested during a private worship service on Sunday in the home of William Witter, with whom they were staying. He was a blind man who had been baptized as a believer. Among the charges against them were conducting an unlawful worship service and speaking against infant baptism. Placed in prison in Boston, all three had fines levied on them with the provision that if the fines were not paid the prisoners would be publicly whipped. The prisoners requested an opportunity to present their case in a disputation, but the request was denied. After many days in prison, Clarke was freed when people paid his fine without his knowledge. Crandall also was freed.

However, Obadiah Holmes refused to pay the fine or to allow others to pay it. Therefore the sentence of public whipping was carried out of thirty strokes with a three-corded whip, the same number that the "worst malefactors that were there punished had."[26] In a letter to friends in London, Holmes described the beating. Excerpts of the letter show the cruelty of his treatment:

> . . . with an audible voyce I brake forth, praying unto the Lord not to lay this Sin to their charge, and telling the people, That now I found he did not fail me, and therefore now I should trust him for ever who failed me not; for in truth, as the stroaks fell upon me, I had such a spirituall manifestation of Gods presence, as the like thereunto I never had, nor felt, nor can with fleshly tongue expresse, and the outward pain was so removed from me, that indeed I am not able to declare it to you, it was so easie to me, that I could well bear it, yea and in a manner felt it not, although it was grievous, as the Spectators said, the Man striking with all his strength (yea spitting on his hand three times, as many affirmed,) with a three-coarded whip, giving me therewith thirty stroaks; when he had loosed me from the Post, having joyfulnesse in my heart, and cheerfulness in my countenance, as the Spectators observed, I told the Magistrates, you have struck me as with Roses.[27]

The news of the brutal beating served to spread the case against religious persecution and rally support for religious freedom. One example of this is the case of Henry Dunster (1612–1659), the first president of Harvard College. When his study of the Bible led him to conclude that infant baptism was unscriptural, he refused to have his child baptized. As a result he was forced to resign as president in 1654. Louis Asher, in a biography of Clarke, states, "Although some disagreement exists as to when President Dunster was converted to Baptist views, others believe that he was so moved by the beating of Holmes and his unflinching acceptance of it that Dunster became a Baptist."[28]

In most of the southern colonies, such as Virginia, the Anglican Church (or Church of England) was the established church. Religious freedom did not exist. Here Baptists encountered discrimination, harassment, and persecution. Fines and imprisonment were used in efforts to curtail believer's baptism and discourage the existence of Baptist churches. Mocking crowds disrupted Baptist worship services and baptisms. Government officials did little or nothing to stop such harassment.

The Baptist Role in Religious Freedom Finally Coming to America

Throughout the 1600s little progress was made toward religious freedom, but the groundwork was being laid for great advance in the 1700s. Baptists contributed significantly to this advance through public testimony, writings, and organizations.

In New England, Isaac Backus (1724–1806) led the way. In Virginia, John Leland (1754–1841) did. But hundreds of others, less well known, contributed to the effort.[29]

Isaac Backus in New England

Isaac Backus, a spiritual product of the Great Awakening that swept across much of colonial America in the early 1700s, served as pastor of a Baptist church in Middleborough, Massachusetts. In addition to serving as pastor of the church, he wrote, preached, lobbied, and formed organizations in behalf of religious freedom. He authored forty-four books and pamphlets. Seven of them were specifically on the topic of religious liberty.[30]

Backus penned a three-volume history of Baptists in New England. In it he recorded at length the persecution that Baptists endured in the first decades of the 1700s, primarily for their refusal to pay the tax levied by the government for the support of the Congregational churches. The government officials in Massachusetts confiscated property and imprisoned men and women on numerous occasions, often for paltry sums of unpaid taxes.

Concerning the issue of taxes for religious purposes in Massachusetts and the Baptist opposition, Thomas J. Curry, a Roman Catholic priest and historian, in his book *The First Freedoms*, states:

> *In theory Massachusetts had long exempted Baptists from paying towards the support of the established churches, but in fact the authorities—particularly after the increase in the number of Baptists there following the Great Awakening—found all kinds of legal loopholes through which to harass them and extract taxes from them for the support of the Congregational system.*[31]

Similar events took place in Connecticut. Backus's mother was home, quite ill, sitting by the fire and reading the family Bible, when officers came to collect the tax, apparently thinking that in her condition she would pay rather than risk arrest. But Mrs. Backus was not about to abandon her religious principles. She refused to pay. She recounts some of that experience in the following excerpts from the letter to her son, Isaac, and also cites other cruelties and injustices:

> *And now I would tell you something of our trials. Your brother Samuel lay in prison twenty days. October 15, the collectors came to our house, and took me away to prison about nine o'clock, in a dark rainy night. Brothers Hill and Sabin were brought there the next night. We lay in prison thirteen days and then set at liberty, by what means I know not. . . . Deacon Griswold was put into prison the 8th of October, and yesterday old brother Grover, and [they] are in pursuit of others; all which calls for humiliation. This church hath appointed the 13th November to be spent in prayer and fasting on that account. . . . These from your loving mother, Elizabeth Backus.*[32]

In 1773 Backus as the "Agent for the Baptists in New England" and a member of the Grievance Committee of the Warren Association urged the churches of New England to adopt a policy of noncompliance with the Exemption Laws related to taxes for the established church. He backed this bold call for civil disobedience with a treatise, *An Appeal to the Public for Religious Liberty, Against the Oppression of the Present Day.* In this publication he made a strong case for religious freedom using Scripture, reason, and examples from history that demonstrated the evils resulting from lack of religious liberty. He declared, "We hope none will. . .expect that spoiling of goods or imprisonment can move us to *betray* the cause of true liberty."[33] In his biography of Backus, William G. McLoughlin states,

> An Appeal to the Public *was pietistic America's declaration of spiritual independence. Like Jefferson's Declaration three years later, it contained a legal brief against a long train of abuses, a theoretical defense of principle, and a moral argument for civil disobedience.*[34]

Backus's arguments for religious freedom contain the sentiments that led the colonies to rebel against England, such as "no taxation without representation." He particularly attacked the use of tax money for the support of churches or religious causes. The historian Brackney reports,

> *In a statement to the Massachusetts legislature in 1774, Backus audaciously quipped, "All America are alarmed at the tea tax; though if they please they can avoid it by not buying the tea; but we have no such liberty (in regard to the church tax). . . . These lines are to let you know, that we are determined not to pay either of them.*[35]

With the support of the Warren Association, Backus took the pleas of the Baptists before the First Continental Congress meeting in Philadelphia in 1774. He hoped that a break with England by the colonies would lead to full religious freedom. After arriving in Philadelphia, Backus and those with him were advised to meet with the official delegation from Massachusetts rather than attempt to speak to the entire Congress.

Following this advice, Backus made his appeal to the delegates to the Congress from Massachusetts. His arguments did not change their commitment to the establishment of the Congregational system. In fact, John Adams, a delegate from Massachusetts, told Backus and the other members of the group appealing for disestablishment that they "might as soon expect a change in the solar system as to expect that they would give up their establishment."[36]

John Leland in Virginia

In the Southern colonies, John Leland and others trumpeted the "cause of true liberty." The passion of Leland's life is indicated in the epitaph on his gravestone: "Here lies the body of John Leland, who labored 67 years to promote piety and vindicate the civil and religious rights of all men."

Leland, as did Backus, advanced the cause of freedom through speaking, writing, and organization, working through the General Committee of Baptists in Virginia. However, he added another dimension to his efforts: relationship and even friendship with political leaders in Virginia who favored religious freedom, particularly Thomas Jefferson and James Madison.

Leland, a native of Massachusetts, ministered in Virginia during the mid 1700s. An effective preacher and writer, he often used humor, vivid language, and sharp wit to present the cause of religious freedom. In evaluating the contribution of Leland to religious freedom, the historian Curry wrote, "Indeed, until Leland no religious thinker matched the thought on Church and State of Roger Williams of the previous century."[37]

The Anglican Church, the established church in Virginia, enjoyed special privileges and support from the government. Tax money paid the Anglican clergy and provided Anglican church buildings. Laws existed to curtail Baptists and other religious groups not part of the established church. The government claimed the right to license preachers and to limit the sphere of their activity. Baptists often refused to obey these laws and consequently were arrested, imprisoned, and fined.

Usually the charge against the preachers was disturbing the peace. In 1768 several Baptist preachers were arrested, hauled before the court, and arraigned as disturbers of the peace. The lawyer bringing the charge against them declared, "May it please your courtships, these men are great disturbers of the peace, they can not meet a man upon the road, but they must ram a passage of Scripture down his throat."[38]

Patrick Henry, the famous lawyer and patriot, on one occasion defended a Baptist preacher who had been arrested for preaching. The fiery orator shouted, "Great God, gentlemen, a man in prison for preaching the gospel of the son of God!"[39] The man was acquitted. Others were not so fortunate. Baptist preachers often were confined in jails for weeks, sometimes without adequate provisions. Frequently they preached through the prison bars to crowds gathered outside.

An example of this treatment is the case of James Ireland, a young Baptist preacher:

> *Ireland was served notice that if he met his appointment to preach the next day, he would be arrested. He says, "I sat down and counted the cost. Freedom or prison? It admitted of no dispute. Having ventured all upon Christ, I determined to suffer all for him." Ireland preached and while praying was arrested and was asked for his authority. He replied, "The author of the Gospel.". . . They were determined to make an example of him and sent him to prison. The rabble surrounded the little jail, deluging him all night with oaths and abuse and showers of sticks and stones through the bars. "A very uncomfortable night," was his restrained comment.*
>
> *Bad as were all eighteenth century jails, the one-room building in Culpeper where Ireland lay from November until April was of the worst, its keeper the most avaricious and heartless, and his persecutors the most outrageous. They abused him with the vilest epithets, reached through the bars to take hold of him, stripped and flogged the Negroes in his audience and practiced unmentionable obscenity to his face as he preached through the little iron gate. They filled the jail with fumes of burning sulphur and pepper, they exploded gun powder under it and formed a plot to poison him. He suffered from a scorching fever and his health was permanently injured.*[40]

In protest of such incidents, Leland argued that the government had no right to make laws that dealt with religion. He declared,

Government has no more to do with the religious opinions of men, than it has with the principles of mathematics. Let every man speak freely without fear, maintain the principle that he believes, worship according to his own faith, either one God, three Gods, no God, or twenty Gods; and let government protect him in so doing.[41]

A number of the political leaders of Virginia were more sympathetic with the Baptist views on religious liberty than the government officials in New England were. For example, Thomas Jefferson (1743–1826) led the fight for the disestablishment of the Episcopal Church in Virginia and the effort to pass the "Virginia Statute Establishing Religious Freedom," which was passed in 1786. Leland and other Baptists were strong supporters of Jefferson in this effort.

When Jefferson was elected president of the United States, Leland took a thousand-pound cheese to Jefferson as a token of gratitude and congratulations. Jefferson's appreciation for the Baptists is evident in letters he wrote to various Baptist groups.[42]

Revolution, Constitution, and the First Amendment

Baptists overwhelmingly supported the Revolution of the colonies against England. The themes of the Revolution, such as freedom, equality, and democracy, fit Baptist beliefs. When the Revolution was finally won, Baptists were disappointed that the new government provided for in the Articles of Confederation made no provision for religious freedom.

When the Articles proved unsatisfactory as a guide for the government of the new nation, a convention was called to draft an improved guiding document. The delegates gathered in the State House, known today as Independence Hall, in Philadelphia in May of 1787. George Washington (1732–1799) was elected to preside over the Convention. At first the delegates attempted to improve the Articles of Confederation, but by mid-June they realized that a totally new guiding document was needed.

Baptists hoped for a provision to guarantee religious freedom. However, no such provision was made in the Constitution that was finally approved in September and recommended by the Convention to the states for ratification. The Constitution required that at least nine of the thirteen states had to ratify the document before it would go into effect.

The process of ratification of the Constitution ushered in an era of fierce controversy. Those in favor of ratification were known as Federalists, mainly because the Constitution established a strong federal government. Those against were known as Anti-federalists. They opposed the Constitution for various reasons, such as a lack of guarantee for certain rights.

The Constitution made no provision guaranteeing religious freedom. Therefore many Baptists opposed ratification. The Baptist role in the ratification process is set forth more fully in the next chapter, but here is a summary.

In Virginia, John Leland and other Baptists campaigned against ratification because of the lack of guarantee for religious freedom. Leland met with James Madison (1751–1836), who was running as a Federalist for the Virginia ratification convention. Leland urged Madison to support publicly an amendment to the Constitution guaranteeing religious freedom. In return Leland promised to support Madison's campaign for ratification. Madison publicly agreed to support an amendment and was elected to the ratification convention in Virginia.

By 1788 the required number of states had ratified the Constitution. In 1789 the new government began to operate. George Washington was elected as president, and the various members of Congress were elected by the states. James Madison was elected as a congressman from Virginia. True to his promise, when Congress first convened Madison led the effort to amend the Constitution by providing a Bill of Rights. As finally passed, the First Amendment guaranteed religious freedom: "Congress shall make no law respecting an establishment of religion, or prohibiting the free exercise thereof."

However, until the ratification of the Fourteenth Amendment in 1868, the First Amendment did not apply to state laws. Therefore, some of the states that had official government-supported churches maintained those establishments.

The "City on the Hill" Versus the "Lively Experiment"

Two major streams of thought regarding church-state relations flowed through early America. One was the Puritan ideal of a Christian society with laws based on the Bible, enforced by a government composed only of church members to establish a "city on the hill" as an example for all to follow. The governor of the Puritan Massachusetts Bay Colony declared that they had a covenant with God and a responsibility to spread this view of society throughout the world.

The other major stream of thought was that of Roger Williams and John Clarke, who established a colony as a "lively experiment" in religious freedom based on separation of church and state. Williams "denounced the 'city on a hill' as a flawed experiment."[43]

These two concepts of church-state relations lived on for years in the American colonies, with initially the church-state union view prevailing. Later the church-state separation view gained official recognition. The two views live on today. Some people clamor for a return to the "city on a hill" while others maintain that the "lively experiment" works wonderfully well for both church and state.

Conclusion

With the adoption of the First Amendment to the Constitution, for the first time in history a national government guaranteed full religious freedom in its laws—not mere toleration, but freedom. The relation of church and state in the United States of America, therefore, broadened "the freedom road."

However, since several of the states maintained established churches, "the freedom road" still needed widening. For religious freedom to exist in all of America, the separation of church and state needed to take place. The story of the development of church-state relations in America and the role of Baptists in that story is the subject of the next chapters.

CHAPTER *Four*

Religious Freedom and Church-State Separation

"Church and state should be separate."

— *BAPTIST FAITH AND MESSAGE*, 1963,
ARTICLE XVII

APTISTS CHAMPION THE CAUSE OF religious freedom. They also contend for the separation of church and state, of the institutions of religion and government. Why? In brief because the relation of religion and government determines the degree of religious freedom.

Through the centuries Baptists have insisted that friendly separation of church and state affords the greatest degree of religious freedom. Historian Slayden Yarbrough observed that for early Baptists, "Religious Liberty and separation of church and state were two sides of the same coin and could not be divided."[1] These Baptists advocated a separation of the institutions of religion and government that was not hostile but neutral or friendly.

For Baptists the separation of church and state is not an end in itself but a means to an end—religious freedom. Actually religious freedom is not the final end sought. Rather it is a means to a genuine, positive relationship with God and an authentic Christian witness and ministry. This chapter examines the issue of church-state relations and the importance of separation to religious freedom.

The Meaning of "Church" and "State"

Baptists have traditionally been loyal citizens. For example, Thomas Helwys in his statement to King James I about religious freedom in *A Short Declaration of the Mistery of Iniquity* wrote that we "profess and teach that in all earthly things the king's power is to be submitted unto. . . ."[2] At the same time Baptists have held firmly to their spiritual values.

This dual commitment as citizens of a nation and citizens of heaven is in large measure due to the Baptist devotion to the authority of the Bible and its teachings about the role of governments and of churches. The Bible sets forth the appropriate functions of both government and church, the desirable relation between the two, and the responsibilities of Christians to each.

Baptists have looked more to the New Testament than to the Old for insight on the roles and relationship of church and state. One reason is that the Old Testament has been used by some to defend the "divine right of kings" and a union of religion and government. Baptists believe these two concepts are no longer applicable in light of New Testament teachings.

The Meaning of "State"

The term *state* relates to organizations that exist to govern the citizens or inhabitants of particular areas, such as nations or cities. The Bible indicates that governments are ordained by God to provide law and order (Romans 13:1-5) and that they have the right to levy taxes and other forms of revenue for secular purposes (Matthew 22:17-22; Rom. 13:6-7). Too, government leaders are to act for the benefit of the citizens (1 Peter 2:13-14).

The Bible indicates that Christians are to honor and pray for government officials (1 Timothy 2:1-3; 1 Pet. 2:17); pay taxes (Matt. 22:17-22; Rom. 13:6-7); and obey the government's laws except when obedience would clearly be contrary to God's will (Acts 4:19–20; 5:29). Jesus set forth the responsibility to pay taxes, even to a government that is not ideal, when he said, "Give to Caesar what is Caesar's, and to God what is God's" (Matt. 22:21).

Of this teaching by Jesus, Baptist preacher George Truett (1867–1944) declared,

> *That utterance of Jesus . . . is one of the most revolutionary and history-making utterances that ever fell from those lips divine. That utterance, once for all, marked the divorcement of church and state. It marked a new era for the creeds and deeds of men.*[3]

Over and over again through the centuries Baptists have quoted Jesus' command as a basis for advocating separation of church and state.

The Meaning of "Church"

For purposes of church-state discussion, the term *church* refers to religious organizations. For Baptists, this includes both local congregations and various entities established for religious purposes.

Baptists believe the Bible teaches that churches are to spread the gospel of Jesus Christ (Luke 24:46–47; Acts 1:8), teach doctrine, develop believers (Matt. 28:19–20; Ephesians 4:11–13), and minister in Christ's name (Matt. 25:31–46). Chapter six contains a further discussion of the nature and function of churches.

The Relation of "Church" and "State"

Both church and state have legitimate God-given purposes. Each carries out its purposes using different methods. The church follows a voluntary pattern. The very nature of the gospel requires a voluntary approach; faith cannot be coerced. The nature of the church requires a voluntary approach—voluntary membership, support, and participation. On the other hand, the state uses coercion for legitimate ends. Financial support of government and obedience to laws, for example, are not voluntary but compulsory. Church and state operate in separate realms and with different methods.

Of course, absolute total separation is not possible. Both church and state occupy the same geographical territory. Many people are both citizens of the state and members of a church. Leaders in one are frequently leaders in the other. However, the organization and function of each should remain as separate as possible. The Bible reveals in broad guidelines God's intent for church and state and the relationship between the two.

The roles of church and state, properly carried out, are mutually beneficial. In providing order and safety, the state aids the church in fulfilling its mission without intruding on the content of that mission (consider Paul's missionary travels in Acts 13:1–20:38). The church contributes to a positive social order by helping to develop law-abiding, hard-working, honest citizens (Eph. 4:20–32; 1 Pet. 2:11–17).

The state is not to dictate doctrine, worship style, organization, membership, or leadership to the church. The church is not to seek the power or the financial support of the state for spiritual ends. The church is to rely on the sword of the Spirit, which is the word of God (Eph. 6:17; Hebrews 4:12), and not the sword of the government (Rom. 13:4) in carrying out its mission. The temptation to use the power of government rather than the power of the Spirit to advance the gospel is always present.

The Bible sets forth no specific form of government that is ideal, and Christians have lived under many different types of government. Baptist beliefs based on the Bible support a democratic form of government. The God-given competency of the individual soul, the priesthood of all believers, voluntary church membership, and congregational church governance all contribute to a Baptist affirmation of democracy as a desirable type of government.

The Background of Church-State Relations

The account of the relationship of church and state through the centuries is complex and lengthy and has been described in various ways.[4] In whatever way the relation is described, these facts are clear: religious freedom has been rare, and persecution has been common. In addition to persecution, wars between religious groups have brought widespread pain and bloodshed.

The Act of Toleration in England in 1689 brought most of the harsh persecution there to a halt. However, this resulted only in religious toleration, not full freedom. A few people dared to speak for complete religious freedom. Baptists were among them because Baptists make a distinction between religious toleration and religious freedom and seek the latter. George Truett heralded this truth:

> *Our contention is not for mere toleration, but for absolute liberty. There is a wide difference between toleration and liberty. Toleration implies that somebody falsely claims the right to tolerate. Toleration is a concession, while liberty is a right. Toleration is a matter of expedience, while liberty is a matter of principle. Toleration is a gift from man, while liberty is a gift from God.[5]*

Religious freedom first began to shine in what would become the United States of America. At first it was only a flicker in Rhode Island. The flame of freedom sputtered for more than 150 years until finally it burst forth with the First Amendment, which provided religious freedom through the separation of institutional religion and government. Many people predicted the relationship of separation would bring catastrophe. However, the result has been positive.

Since separation of church and state and full religious freedom were new in the world, many specifics in the relationship had to be worked out. The ideal is clear. The particulars have not always been that clear. Dynamic changes in society have called for continued clarification and adjustment. Let's take a look at the role Baptists have played in the development of church-state relations and religious freedom.

The Origins of Church-State Separation in America

As people from Europe began to explore and settle in the New World, they brought with them the church-state patterns that existed in the

Old World, which have been described in preceding chapters. The colonies generally had some vestige of church-state union.

Early Church-State Relations in Colonial America

Only the colony of Rhode Island, established by Roger Williams and John Clarke, was based on full religious liberty. Williams believed religious liberty "depended on complete separation of church and state."[6] Thus, from the very beginning of their existence in America, Baptists advocated separation of church and state as a means of providing religious freedom, not just for themselves but for all people.

One of the leading early Baptist advocates for freedom was Williams's co-worker in Rhode Island, John Clarke. (See chapter three under the heading "The Early Baptist Role in Religious Freedom in America.") The colony lacked an official charter, and Clarke and Williams sailed for England in 1651 to acquire one. Williams returned to the colony, but Clarke remained in England. Clarke petitioned the government a number of times to obtain "the first legal guarantee of individual liberty of conscience in matters of faith and worship."[7] In that petition he wrote that one of the purposes of the colony was "TO HOLD FORTH A LIVELY EXPERIMENT THAT A MOST FLOURISHING CIVILL STATE MAY STAND . . . AND BEST BE MAINTAYNED . . . WITH A FULL LIBERTIE IN RELIGIOUS CONCERNMENTS."[8] Finally, in 1663, "the long awaited patent was passed under King Charles's seal."[9]

As previous chapters have indicated, during the next century Baptists such as Isaac Backus and John Leland continued the Baptist effort for freedom. In spite of the campaign by Baptists and others, by the time of the American Revolution in 1776 full religious freedom remained only a hope and not a reality.

Arguments for Religious Liberty and Separation of Church and State

Baptists participated in the Revolutionary War, fighting against English rule and supporting the cause of independence. The themes of the Revolution, such as liberty and freedom, had been part of the Baptist fabric for years. So Baptists rallied to the cause. They fought against the king's army, marching side by side with people from the established churches that persecuted them.

This sacrifice for the cause of freedom is reflected in a statement from the General Committee of Baptists in Virginia to the Virginia Assembly in 1786: "For this free government we advanced our property and exposed our lives on the field of battle with our fellow Citizens; being often Stimulated with the harmonious Proclamation of equal Liberty of conscience and equal claim of property."[10]

Baptists hoped that when independence was achieved, the cause of freedom would include religious freedom. Such hope proved to be ill-founded. The new nation under the Articles of Confederation provided no guarantee of religious freedom. Established state churches continued to impose both taxes and restrictions on the freedom of Baptists and others.

The Constitution drafted in 1787 replaced the ineffectual Articles of Confederation but contained no provision for religious freedom. The only hint of religious liberty was the provision in Article VI that there should be no religious test for holding office in the new nation.

When the Constitution was placed before the states for ratification, Baptists were among those most vocal in opposition unless an amendment could be made to provide for religious freedom. The inclusion of such an amendment resulted from efforts by a divergent group of people, with Baptists among the leaders.

In addition to Baptists, early advocates of freedom of religion in the colonies included Quakers, Mennonites, and many Presbyterians. Thomas Jefferson and James Madison, members of the established church in Virginia, the Anglican church, were the most vocal and active political leaders for religious freedom and separation of church and state.

People argued for separation of church and state and religious freedom from different perspectives. For example, as mentioned earlier, Roger Williams wrote of a "hedge or wall of separation between the Garden of the Church and the Wilderness of the world."[11] Thomas Jefferson, in his letter to the Danbury Baptist Association, wrote of a "wall of separation between church and state." Mark DeWolfe Howe, writing on American constitutional history in *The Garden and The Wilderness*, comments about these two references to separation that

> *the metaphor as it came from the pen of Jefferson carried a very different overtone of conviction from that which it bore in the message of Williams. The principle of separation epitomized in Williams' metaphor was predominantly theological. The principle summarized in the same figure when used by Jefferson was primarily political.*[12]

For Baptists, the belief in religious freedom and separation of church and state rested on basic biblical beliefs. Baptists did not discount reason or the lessons learned from history. But for them revelation was even more basic. God's revelation in the Bible of the nature of God, humankind, salvation, and church led Baptists to contend for freedom of religion.

For example, in 1786 the General Committee of Baptists in Virginia in a formal statement to the General Assembly of Virginia declared, "New Testament Churches, we humbly conceive, are, or should be, established by the Legislature of Heaven and not earthly power; by the Law of God and not the Law of the State; by the acts of the Apostles and not by the Acts of an Assembly."[13] And Backus's biographer says of him, "Like a true pietist, he placed as much reliance upon Biblical texts as upon the works of Locke to prove the necessity for separation of Church and State."[14] Historian Walter Shurden expressed a similar Baptist sentiment: "Freedom is more than a constitutional right or government gift. God, not nations or courts or human law, is the ultimate source of liberty."[15]

On the other hand, leaders who were part of the Enlightenment, or the Age of Reason, such as Jefferson, took a different approach based primarily on observation and reason. Those who held Enlightenment views had a deep faith, not in traditional Christian revelation, but in human reason. Logic and observation convinced them that genuine religious belief could not be coerced. Coercion, they contended, might lead to some sort of outward confession of belief but not to genuine belief. Thus they argued that governments ought not use coercion in matters of belief and faith.

As John Witte concludes in *Religion and the American Constitutional Experiment,* "Both views were united, however, in their opposition to the traditional . . . alliances of church and state."[16] Baptists welcomed these allies in the struggle for freedom.

Why make such a point about the differences and similarities between the Baptists and the politicians? For one reason, Baptists need to remember always that the Baptist commitment to the separation of church and state preceded the First Amendment. The Baptist devotion to religious liberty and church-state separation is part of the *Baptist DNA* and not just eighteenth-century political theory.

Nevertheless, the First Amendment is very significant. And the Baptist role in developing it is very interesting. The story in brief is as follows.

Baptists, the First Amendment, Religious Freedom, and Church-State Separation

Baptists in pre-revolutionary America had blanketed the colonies with appeals for religious freedom and church-state separation. People such as Thomas Jefferson and James Madison agreed with the Baptist position on these issues.

Thomas Jefferson and the Baptists. Jefferson was not only the primary author of the Declaration of Independence in 1776 but also of the Virginia Statute for Religious Freedom. He was particularly proud of the latter because it set forth his views on religious freedom and the need for church-state separation. When it became law in 1786, Virginia became "the first government in the world to establish by statute the complete divorce of Church and State,—the greatest contribution of America to the sum of Western civilization."[17] Rhode Island had separation of church and state more than a hundred years earlier, but by charter and not by formal statute as in Virginia.

Jefferson wrote in his autobiography that he desired all religions to have freedom from coercion: "The Jew and the Gentile, the Christian and Mahometan, the Hindoo, and infidel of every denomination."[18] Roger Williams had expressed a similar sentiment more than a century earlier: "It is the will and command of God that, since

the coming of his Son the Lord Jesus, a permission of the most Pagan-
ish, Jewish, Turkish, or anti-Christian consciences and worships be
granted to all men in all nations and countries. . . ."[19]

The Baptists enjoyed a positive relationship with Jefferson. An
aunt of Jefferson was a member of the Buck Mountain Baptist Church
near Monticello, Jefferson's home. It was this church "tradition says
Jefferson pronounced 'an admirable model for a Republic.'"[20] In a
Baptist church he could view democracy in action, common folks
governing themselves.

Jefferson expressed appreciation to the Baptists for their con-
sistent stand for religious freedom. Jefferson penned the term "wall
of separation between church and state" while he was president of
the United States in a letter to the Danbury Baptist Association of
Connecticut:

> *Believing with you that religion is a matter which lies solely between*
> *Man & his God, that he owes account to none other for his faith or his*
> *worship, that the legitimate powers of government reach actions only,*
> *& not opinions, I contemplate with sovereign reverence that act of the*
> *whole American people which declared that their legislature should*
> *"make no law respecting an establishment of religion, or prohibiting*
> *the free exercise thereof," thus building a wall of separation between*
> *Church & State.*[21]

He also expressed gratitude to Baptist associations in Virginia for the
Baptist support of religious freedom.[22]

Commenting on the "wall," Leonard Levy, a scholar whose spe-
cialty is the Constitution and the Bill of Rights, wrote, "Despite its
detractors and despite its leaks, cracks, and its archways, the wall
ranks as one of the mightiest monuments of constitutional government in this nation."[23] The "wall" statement by Jefferson has been
used in decisions of the United States Supreme Court and by numerous people discussing church-state relations.

James Madison and the Baptists. James Madison was another staunch
advocate of religious freedom through church-state separation. He is
often regarded as one of the primary architects of the Constitution.

He too had a relation with and appreciation for the Baptists. John Leland is credited with influence on Madison, especially in relation to the Constitution and the First Amendment. On two occasions Leland aided Madison in political campaigns, first when Madison was a candidate for the Virginia convention to ratify the Constitution and second when Madison ran for Congress under the new Constitution.

The Constitution as approved by the Constitutional Convention in 1787 contained a provision that it would not become the law of the land until at least nine of the states had ratified it. The ratification process was through delegates selected within each state to a special meeting in the state to consider ratification. Madison ran as a delegate for ratification in Virginia.

The Baptists in Virginia were deeply disappointed that the Constitution provided no guarantee for religious freedom. Therefore, many Baptists opposed ratification. John Leland, pastor in Orange County, was one of the leaders of the opposition. Leland "came out as candidate from that strongly Baptist county for the Virginia convention, in opposition to its ratification of the Constitution and against Madison, who favored it."[24]

Word came to Madison that ratification of the Constitution by Virginia was in jeopardy because of the Baptist opposition led by Leland. Captain Joseph Spencer, a Baptist who had served time in prison for his faith, urged Madison to come to Virginia and visit with the Baptists and especially with John Leland. Spencer encouraged Madison to assure them of his commitment to religious freedom and to campaign for ratification. Richard Labunski in his biography of Madison states, "If Leland had doubts about the new government and could not be persuaded to support it, Madison's election to the Richmond convention was in danger."[25]

Madison was in New York, then the site of the national government. He was not eager to travel to Virginia, but with further urging he agreed to come. Arriving in Virginia, he met with Leland and other Baptists in Orange County, a center of opposition to ratification.[26] Madison reassured them of his strong commitment to religious freedom. After Madison had "fully and unreservedly communicated to him his opinions, Leland, at a gathering of the voters at Gum Spring, announced his support of Madison, who was then elected without difficulty."[27] Virginia ratified the Constitution. Madison and Leland remained friends as evidenced by correspondence between them in following years.[28]

Baptists also played a role in Massachusetts in the ratification of the Constitution. Isaac Backus was elected as a delegate from Middleborough to the ratification convention meeting in Boston in 1788. When the convention convened, the majority of the delegates seemed opposed to ratification, including the twenty Baptists who were delegates. Backus became convinced that ratification was best and spoke in favor of that position. The final vote was close: 187 for and 168 against, a majority of only 19, with the influence of Backus evident.[29]

With the Constitution ratified, the new government was formed with George Washington as president. Baptists were concerned that religious liberty would not be guaranteed. The Bill of Rights had not yet been introduced. The General Committee of Baptists in Virginia wrote a letter to Washington, their fellow Virginian, indicating their reservations about the Constitution.

The letter expressed that Washington's accepting the presidency eased their concerns:

> But amidst all the inquititudes of mind, our consolation arose from this consideration, the plan must be good, for it bears the signature of a tried, trusty friend; and if religious liberty is rather insecure in the Constitution "the administration will certainly prevent all oppression, for a WASHINGTON will preside."[30]

Washington replied with an assurance of his commitment to religious freedom: "I beg you will be persuaded, that *no one would be more zealous than myself to establish effectual barriers against the horrors of spiritual tyranny, and every species of religious persecution.*"[31]

Madison had promised to introduce an amendment to the Constitution that would guarantee religious freedom. In order to do so, he had to be elected to the first Congress. For the second time, he faced serious opposition from Baptists in his candidacy. In his account of *James Madison and the Bill of Rights*, Labunski states,

Several groups in the district needed to be assured that Madison was genuinely committed to working for a bill of rights. Baptists, who would play a crucial role in the election, wanted Madison's pledge that he believed an amendment protecting religious freedom was necessary and he would work toward its approval in Congress.[32]

Madison used several methods to convince Baptists and other voters of his commitment to an amendment providing religious freedom. One of these methods was to write letters intended for wide circulation. Labunski comments, "The most important of the letters was the one he wrote on January 2 to the Reverend George Eve, a Baptist minister and the pastor of the Blue Run Church of Orange County."[33] The importance that Madison ascribed to Eve is seen in his opening sentence:

Being informed that reports prevail not only that I am opposed to any amendments whatever to the new federal Constitution; but that I have ceased to be a friend to the rights of Conscience; and inferring from a conversation with my brother William, that you are disposed to contradict such reports as far as your knowledge of my sentiments may justify, I am led to trouble you with this communication of them.

Madison further stated in the letter,

It is my sincere opinion that the Constitution ought to be revised, and that the first Congress meeting under it ought to prepare and recommend to the States for ratification, the most satisfactory provisions for all essential rights, particularly the rights of Conscience in the fullest latitude, the freedom of the press, trials by jury, security against general warrants &c.[34]

Madison's letter to Eve convinced the pastor of Madison's sincerity. In a meeting to discuss the candidates for Congress, Madison's views were attacked, and Eve defended Madison. In a report of the meeting to Madison, a participant in the meeting wrote,

*Mr. Eve took a very Spirited and decided Part in your favor, he Spoke
Long on the Subject, and reminded them of the many important Ser-
vices which you had rendered. . . .in particular the Act for establishing
Religious Liberty [in the Virginia Declaration of Rights]. . . .*[35]

For several reasons Madison was reluctant to come to Virginia
from New York, where he was serving in the Congress under the Articles of Confederation. He explained to George Washington that he
was suffering from a physical condition that made travel very uncom-
fortable.[36] However, he went to Virginia, campaigned personally, and
pledged he would work for a bill of rights with a guarantee of religious freedom.

In Madison's campaign for Congress, he again sought the support of John Leland, the Virginia Baptist leader.[37] Leland, of course,
had earlier helped Madison be elected to the ratifying convention.
Madison again was successful in gaining Leland's favor. When Madison was elected, Leland wrote him a letter congratulating him and
stating, "One Thing I shall expect; that if religious Liberty is anywise
threatened, that I shall receive the earliest Intelligence. I take the Liberty of writing this to you, lest I should not be at Home when you
pass by on your way to Congress."[38]

On his election to the first Congress, Madison presented a series
of amendments to the Constitution. One of these as finally ratified
provided for religious freedom. Significantly the amendment recognized the close relationship of religious freedom with freedom
of speech, assembly, and the press. In a sense, religious freedom
depends on these other freedoms, and they depend on religious
freedom.

After various wordings were considered and conferences were
held between members of the House and the Senate, what is now
termed the First Amendment was finalized:

*Congress shall make no law respecting an establishment of religion, or
prohibiting the free exercise thereof; or abridging the freedom of speech,
or of the press; or the right of the people peaceably to assemble, and to
petition the Government for a redress of grievances.*

The First Amendment did not eliminate all government-estab-lished churches in the United States. Because certain powers were reserved for the states, some, such as Massachusetts, retained their established churches. John Leland returned to his native Massachu-setts in 1791 and labored there for separation of church and state. Finally, in 1833, he lived to see the Congregational Church system disestablished.

The Meaning of Separation of Church and State

Exactly what did the early Baptists mean by the concept of separation of church and state? What did the Founding Fathers of the United States of America, in the Constitution and the Bill of Rights, intend the relation of church and state to be? The answers to these questions have been debated ever since the adoption of the Constitution and Bill of Rights. They are still hot topics today. Some of the meanings are fairly clear. Others are not.[39]

C. Emanuel Carlson, after a lifetime of study on church-state rela-tions from a Baptist perspective including being the Executive Director of the Baptist Joint Committee on Public Affairs, wrote: "The two insti-tutions must exist and work out their programs in the same chronology, the same localities, with more or less the same people, experiencing the impact of the same current events. Out of this unavoidable fact arise many of the problems in church-state relations."[40]

Although Baptists hold different views on what should be the exact relation of church and state, most agree on the concept of sepa-ration. For example, several major Baptist groups in the United States set forth in 1959 these understandings of the separation of church and state: "*Separate reasons for being. . . . Separate publics. . . . Distinct methods. . . . Separate administration. . . . Separate sources of support. . . . Separate educational programs.*"[41]

Baptists differ about the degree of separateness. Some are very strict separationists. Others are less so.

Baptists as well as the drafters of the Constitution and Bill of Rights clearly intended that there be institutional separation of church and state. Organized religion should not dictate to the government matters regarding basic civic laws. Governments should not dictate to religious groups or to individuals matters regarding spiritual issues such as religious doctrine, church organization, and worship. The government should not collect taxes for the support of religious institutions or use general tax funds for the financing of religious institutions.

Furthermore, the relation of government to religious organizations was to be neutral, even friendly. The separation intended by the founders of the nation was not to be like that of the Soviet Union, for example. The Soviet constitution stated specifically that there was to be the separation of church and state. However, that separation was unfriendly, leading to persecution of many religious groups.

Results of the Separation of Church and State

The separation of church and state in the United States was referred to, even by its early advocates, as an experiment. No nation had ever attempted to do this before. No one was sure how it would work out. Many questions existed about such a relationship. These questions had to be considered as changes in both organized religion and governments occurred through the years. Various people and groups understood *separation* in different ways, and the differences had to be dealt with.

The Concerns about Separation of Church and State

Those who opposed the separation of church and state expressed many concerns at the beginning of the experiment in the life of the nation. *Some expressed fear that disestablishment of churches would lead to the demise of religion in American life.* They doubted that voluntary support would ever be adequate to pay clergy and to maintain facilities. The fear proved to be ill-founded. Under the freedom provided by separation of church and state, religious life in America has thrived.

For example, in 1818, the Congregational Church system was disestablished in Connecticut. The well-known Congregational minister, Lyman Beecher, indicated that he expected the results of disestablishment to be catastrophic. Later he freely admitted that just the opposite was true. He said that the separation of the church from support by the state benefited both. Concerning the disestablishment Beecher wrote,

> *The injury done to the cause of Christ, as we then supposed, was irreparable. For several days I suffered what no tongue can tell* for the best that ever happened to the State of Connecticut. *It cut the church loose from dependence on state support. It threw them wholly on their own resources and on God.*
>
> *They say ministers have lost their influence; the fact is, they have gained.* [42]

A few years later Alexis de Tocqueville, a French Catholic, observed American life extensively and concluded, "Far from suffering from want of state support, religion seems in the United States to stand all the firmer because, standing alone, she is seen to stand by her own strength."[43] That observation would be true today.

Another concern was that separation would lead to immorality in society and instability in government. The belief held by many was that morality and stability depend on a union of religion and government. This was the prevailing view of Christendom during the Middle Ages—a view that led to persecution and war rather than to moral perfection or social stability.

Again this fear has proved to be ill-founded. Under friendly separation both government and religion have flourished. In a letter to Robert Walsh in 1819 James Madison observed,

> *It was the Universal opinion of the Century preceding the last, that Civil Govt. could not stand without the prop of a Religious establishment, & that the Xn. Religion itself, would perish if not supported by a legal provision for its Clergy. The experience of Virginia conspicuously corroborates the disproof of both opinions. The Civil Govt. tho' bereft of*

*everything like an associated hierarchy possesses the requisite stability
and performs its functions with complete success.*[44]

Waves of social reform, often led by church groups, have swept
through America. Evils such as slavery, abusive child labor, racial
injustice, and lack of women's rights, all of which existed at the
nation's founding, have been swept away. To be sure, America is no
moral utopia, but neither are those countries that have a vestige of
church-state union. America is plagued with many forms of immorality. However, a nation's moral quality depends on the character of its
citizens, not on religious coercion by government. The basic way to
a better society is through changed hearts and not through changed
laws. Good laws are important, but changed lives through the gospel
are more important. That comes through persistent prayer and fervent evangelism.

A third concern was that separation would lead to religious anarchy.
Opponents to separation contended that without the constraining
arm of government, scores, even hundreds, of religious groups would
emerge and engage in a virtual war with each other. They feared that
this would lead to perpetual disruption in the country, resulting in
harm to every area of life, including business.

Many religious groups do indeed exist in America; some have
recently developed and are native to our country. Too, religious
organizations have at times attacked the views of others while
defending their own. Unfortunately the conflicts have sometimes
involved physical assaults. Usually, though, the differences have
been limited to the verbal exchanges guaranteed by freedom of
speech, assembly, and press. Admittedly, the verbiage has sometimes been harsh, even short on truth. But the arrangement of
church-state separation has proved to be beneficial to religion and
not harmful to society as a whole.

*Another concern was that separation would result in a government
that was completely devoid of religion.* The many religious symbols and
expressions evident in the various levels of government in this country demonstrate that this fear has not materialized.

The Benefits of Separation of Church and State

Questions and differences of opinion about separation of church and state still exist. Yet the experiment has worked and is working. Under the relation of neutral or friendly separation, freedom of religion has been achieved to a degree never realized before in history. On the whole, individuals and religious groups enjoy a marvelous degree of freedom in America.

Denominations and religious organizations of various kinds have experienced phenomenal growth. The media is filled with religious preaching and teaching. The internet provides an abundance of religious information. Printed material on religion is readily available. Buildings for religious worship exist in abundance throughout the land. Religious schools, benevolent institutions, hospitals, and ministries of various kinds thrive. Missionaries have been sent throughout the world. In nations where government-established churches continued to exist, religious life has tended to decline in contrast to what has occurred with the friendly separation of church and state in America

Conclusion

Thus the grand experiment of religious freedom under the friendly separation of church and state as envisioned by Baptists and the Founding Fathers of our nation has provided a blessing for both church and state. Indeed, America has been and is the "sweet land of liberty."[45]

With the adoption of the new Constitution and the Bill of Rights, the freedom that had been in tiny Rhode Island a "lively experiment" with separation of church and state became a fixed part of the American scene. Yet, in a sense, the experiment was to continue. "The freedom road" would take many twists and turns and encounter numerous obstacles and difficulties as the years unfolded in the new Republic. That is the subject of the next chapter.

> *"You, my brothers, were called to be free. But do not use your freedom to indulge the sinful nature; rather, serve one another in love."*
>
> GALATIANS 5:13

CHAPTER *Five*

Church-State Separation: A Continuing Challenge

> "There will, of course, remain a borderland where it will not always be clear how to discriminate and apply the principle correctly."
>
> — EDGAR YOUNG MULLINS[1]
> (1860–1928) Baptist theologian
> Statesman and author

THE FRIENDLY SEPARATION OF CHURCH and state as envisioned by Baptists in early America and by the founders of the nation helped make religious freedom a reality in the United States. The preservation of that freedom depends to a large extent on the preservation of the separation of church and state. After years of research and study Leo Pfeffer, jurist and church-state scholar, concluded that "religious freedom is most secure where church and state are separate, and least secure where church and state are united."[2]

The preservation of separation of church and state in turn depends on understanding what separation means and how it is to be applied in a constantly changing society. Such efforts provide a continuing and controversial challenge in determining where the border between church and state ought to be. Well-informed people who believe in religious freedom differ on exactly what the relation of church and state ought to be.

Changes that Challenge Separation

Most people in the United States believe in religious freedom, but many disagree on how church-state separation relates to it. Controversy has always surrounded the relation of church and state, of religion and government. However, the amount of controversy in the United States has increased in recent years due to several factors, such as the following.

The Relative Newness of Church-State Separation

In the broad scope of history, the "lively experiment" launched by Roger Williams and John Clarke in colonial Rhode Island is still in its infancy. When the United States separated church and state, no other nation existed that could serve as a model to follow. Full religious freedom and not mere toleration was an experiment.

From the beginning of the experiment, issues existed that had to be confronted without benefit of prior experience. In a sense, the new nation was feeling its way along an uncharted path. With a diverse population, both in religious beliefs and political theory, decisions defining church-state relations were often controversial. They still are.

Increase in Size and Complexity of Both Government and Institutional Religion

In the early days of our nation, both government and church organizations were relatively small in size and in number. As these grew, they began to intersect more and more with one another. For example, in the beginning of the nation, education was carried out primarily either by individuals or by religious organizations. When government entered the field of education, church-state issues emerged.

What occurred in the field of education also took place in other areas of institutional life in the United States, such as health and charity care. "The American Baptist Bill of Rights," adopted by a number of Baptist bodies in the United States and published in 1940, noted, "The philanthropic activities of the churches within the United States are being taken over by the government."[3] Since that time both the government and the churches have expanded efforts in these fields.

The expansion of both government and church-related interests in education, welfare, medical care, and research has led to increased entanglement of church and state. The church-state issues created by such increased entanglement are numerous.

Rapidly Expanding Diversity of the Population

According to a scholarly work on church and state in the past three centuries in the United States, "Pluralism—of both religions and governments—has been a critical force in the continual reshaping of church-state issues, from the founding period to the present day."[4] The nation was religiously diverse when first established, but the diversity was relatively small, comprised mainly in differences among various Christian denominations. Today the population includes people from practically every world religion and those of none. Not all of these religions have a basic commitment to religious freedom.

To compound the church-state challenge, the increasing diversity of religious expressions makes determining what really is *religion* more and more difficult. Some legal experts even contend that religion "can no longer be coherently defined for purposes of American law."[5] If indeed this is the case (and many legal experts believe it is not), it creates a major church-state issue. The courts must determine what is truly religion and what is not, something the Founding Fathers certainly wanted to avoid.[6]

Real or Perceived Threats to the Nation and Way of Life

Some of the threats to the United States have been from *outside the nation*. One of the responses to such dangers has been to increase the religious expression of the government. For example, when the United States was locked in a deadly struggle with atheistic Communism, the words "under God' in the Pledge of Allegiance to the flag were added in 1954;[7] Congress voted in 1956 for "In God We Trust" to be the official national motto; and in 1957 United States paper currency began to carry the motto.

Some threats to national existence have come from *within the nation*. Heightened emphasis on religion by government leaders has usually been a response. For example, when the United States was torn asunder by the Civil War, President Lincoln often referred to God and quoted the Bible in his speeches. During that terrible war the hymn the "Battle Hymn of the Republic" was written and is often sung at government-sponsored functions.[8]

A shift in the moral values and practices of the nation has resulted in a call by some people for more government support of religion. For example, during the last half of the twentieth century many people in the nation began to experience major social and moral changes that were contrary to traditional Christian values. These developments have been blamed by some on the Supreme Court decisions involving church-state issues. The charge has been made that the Supreme Court is rooting God out of public life. As a result, attacks are made on church-state separation, and appeals are made for more government support of religion.

Could it be that the real cure for declining morality is not government-sponsored religion but genuine spiritual revival? As historian William Estep declared,

> *The moral failure of modern society, as evidenced by the dissolution of the family, drug addiction, sexual immorality accompanied by wholesale abortion, and white-collar crime, is not the result of the freedom provided by the Constitution and the Bill of Rights, but rather a consequence of the failure of those who are called in the name of Christ to live out the gospel as committed disciples both within the community of faith of which they are part and within the society in which they are called to act out the faith.*[9]

Moral Issues Involving Government Legislation or Court Decisions

Issues such as abortion, capital punishment, the nature of marriage, homosexuality, and medical research command increasing attention. People hold strong and divergent views on such issues, and many of these views are based on religious convictions. Since these issues involve public actions and not merely private convictions, governments have been involved in legislation and enforcement. Many of the laws have been challenged, and the resulting court decisions have often been controversial. Church-state questions are front and center in a number of these issues.

Some people contend that governments ought not to become involved because such actions bring government enforcement on behalf of particular religious groups. Others insist that religious groups ought not to endeavor to bring influence on the governments regarding these issues because to do so violates church-state separation.

Although Baptists are divided in their convictions about some of the issues, they are almost unanimous in their opinion that all people, regardless of their religious persuasion, have a right to express their views and to lobby to influence government. Baptists have argued rather consistently that such efforts do not violate church-state separation.

Areas of Controversy Related to Separation

The various changes in America since the adoption of the Constitution and the First Amendment have caused almost constant controversy over how these primary documents for our nation are to be interpreted. People under our form of government are free to believe whatever they want. No government agency is to endeavor to compel belief.

However, when beliefs are translated into actions and organizations, questions often arise about how the principle of church-state separation applies to them. Church-state separation issues have been especially prominent in the following areas. These are only samples of such issues and by no means a comprehensive listing. They do, however, highlight the complexity of church-state issues.

Education

Education has been a battleground for church-state issues for many years. One aspect of the struggle focuses on *government aid for religious schools*. When the Roman Catholic Church was the primary provider of religious elementary and secondary schools and endeavored to get tax support for the schools, their efforts were opposed by most other religious groups as well as secular organizations. Now that thousands of religious schools are operated by other church groups, including Baptists, opposition has wavered. Even some Baptists advocate government aid to religious schools, most often in the form of vouchers.

Another church-state education issue centers on *religious practices in public schools*. The Supreme Court has ruled that government-sponsored prayers, worship services, and devotional Bible reading in public schools are unconstitutional. Those opposed to the rulings have taken several actions. They have established a vast number of private schools where Christian activities can take place, endeavored to get Christian activities and curriculum content into the public schools, lobbied to have laws passed that provide for religion in the public schools, and worked to overturn the Court's decisions.

The *content of curriculum in public schools* is also a point of bitter dispute. Almost every aspect of the curriculum is involved, including science, history, literature, and health. According to law, none of these is to be taught in public schools from a religious point of view. Schools can teach about religion, objectively and fairly, when appropriate in the curriculum, however.

Health

A number of church-state issues relate to health. Certain medical procedures, such as blood transfusions, violate the religious beliefs of Jehovah's Witnesses. Should their children be given transfusions, even over the protest of parents, if such transfusions are necessary to save life? Handling poisonous snakes is an integral part of the worship service of some religions. Should this be allowed?

When religious denominations foster institutions for medical care, they encounter numerous government regulations. Are these a violation of church-state separation? Furthermore, denominational health care institutions receive payments from the government for the care of patients, enjoy tax exemption on property and income, and obtain grants for research. Are these counter to church-state separation?

Marriage and Family

Traditionally laws of various kinds have controlled different aspects of marriage and family life. Monogamy has been the rule of law. However, certain religious groups in our country allow for polygamy. Does making polygamy illegal violate the religious freedom of such groups?

The care, education, and protection of children fall under various governmental regulations. Certainly child abuse is to be neither tolerated nor excused on religious grounds, but what about compulsory standards for education and other government-mandated issues related to children in families?

Benevolence and Human Welfare

Many religious groups are involved in charitable care of people in need. Child care facilities, for example, have been maintained by numerous denominations. Should these institutions accept government funds for the care of children? If so, should they be allowed to provide sectarian religious instruction for the children?

Similarly, when religious organizations distribute food and clothing for the poor, provide shelter for the homeless, and care for the needs of people harmed by natural disasters, should government funds be provided for these activities? If so, should the religious organizations be allowed to carry out sectarian religious teaching to those being helped?

Patriotism and National Defense

Various religious convictions and practices seem in conflict with the nation's interest in patriotism, loyalty, and defense. For example, to require Jehovah's Witnesses to salute and give the Pledge of Allegiance to the flag violates their religious convictions. Should they be compelled to take part in this ceremony?

Some people are pacifists or conscientious objectors to war on the basis of religious convictions. If the numbers of such people were large enough to undermine national defense, would compelling military service for them violate religious freedom? On similar grounds, some pacifists have refused to pay taxes used to finance the military. Does requiring them to pay violate their religious freedom?

Government Property and Religious Symbols and Practices

What are the valid uses of government property for religious purposes? Having manger scenes at Christmas on government property and posting the Ten Commandments in government buildings are among the church-state issues that relate to the use of government property for religious purposes.

A highly emotional issue involving religious symbols on government property involves the markers that carry religious symbols in national cemeteries for the military. Some have challenged the use of such symbols as a church-state violation. Adding to the complexity of this particular matter, the government determines which religious symbols can be used, thus, in a sense, deciding which religions are valid and which are not.

Some people argue that religious symbols on public property are constitutional if all religions have equal access. But would equal access possibly lead to an unmanageable number of religious symbols in government buildings? Similarly, some people contend that if secular and sacred symbols are given equal visibility, this satisfies constitutional requirements for church-state separation.

The Ongoing Role of the Courts

Who is to decide the legality or constitutionality of actions and issues such as those mentioned in the above areas? The United States is a nation governed by law and not by the whims of dictators or the edicts of monarchs. The supreme law of the land is the Constitution. It provides for three branches of government: executive, legislative, and judicial. Each of these relates to church-state matters in some way.

According to Section III of the Constitution, however, the interpretation of laws as related to their constitutionality is the responsibility of the judicial branch. Courts at all levels of government have been involved in church-state cases. The United States Supreme Court is the ultimate authority.

The Supreme Court and Separation of Church and State

As law professor Robert T. Miller has pointed out, "A sobering responsibility rests upon the judiciary in interpreting and delimiting religious freedom and in locating the proper boundary between church and state."[10] Thus issues such as those noted in the preceding sections have been dealt with by the courts, including the United States Supreme Court.

In disputes over the relation of church and state, various sources have been cited, such as the Mayflower Compact, the Declaration of Independence, the Articles of Confederation, writings by the nation's founders, and opinions of learned jurists and academicians. Although these may be interesting and even somewhat instructive, none of them is authoritative. Under our system of government, only the Constitution is of supreme legal authority.

The Constitution as originally ratified contained only one article specifically related to religion, Article VI, Clause 3: "No religious Test shall ever be required as a Qualification to any Office or public Trust of the United States." Many states maintained religious tests for public office within the state, but eventually the constitutional requirement for no religious test was applied by the United States Supreme Court to the states.

The First Amendment contains two provisions regarding religious freedom: "Congress shall make no law respecting an establishment of religion, or prohibiting the free exercise thereof." The first provision is usually referred to as the establishment clause and the second as the free exercise clause. No definitions or specific instructions for application of these provisions are provided in the Constitution. These were left to future generations to determine. As Richard Henry Lee of Virginia noted, they were statements "for ages and nations yet unborn."[11]

When initially passed, the First Amendment related only to actions by the federal government, not those of the states. The Fourteenth Amendment, ratified in 1868, gradually was interpreted to bring the guarantees of the First Amendment to the states. However, it was not until 1940 that religion was clearly included by the Supreme Court within the protection of the Fourteenth Amendment.[12] In that year a unanimous opinion written by Justice Roberts declared:

> *The fundamental concept of liberty embodied in that Amendment [the 14th] embraces the liberties guaranteed by the First Amendment. The First Amendment declares that Congress shall make no law respecting an establishment of religion or prohibiting the free exercise thereof. The Fourteenth Amendment has rendered the legislatures of the states as incompetent as Congress to enact such laws.*[13]

Of this significant milestone in the history of the Supreme Court and church-state separation, John T. Noonan, Jr., who has been both a law professor and a federal judge, wrote, "Prior to 1940 the Supreme Court of the United States had never ... applied the religion clauses of the First Amendment to the states. ... Beginning in 1940 the Court changed all that. It applied the religion clauses to the states."[14]

The U. S. Supreme Court has addressed both the establishment clause and the free exercise clause. Sometimes the two seem to be in tension, and the Court has struggled with the tension.

Commenting on these two clauses, Brent Walker, an attorney specializing in church-state law, has written:

These two clauses, no establishment and free exercise, working together require government to be neutral toward religion, neither advancing nor inhibiting it, but turning it loose to flourish or flounder on its own. Accordingly, government may accommodate religion, but without advancing it; protect religion, but without privileging it; lift burdens on the exercise of religion, but without extending religion an impermissible benefit.[15]

For example, the Supreme Court in deliberating the religion clauses has recognized that "religion and religious institutions often are and should be extended special *concessions* to lift the burdens on the exercise of religion. . . . On the other hand sometimes religion must endure unique *constraints* to ensure compliance with Establishment Clause values."[16] Special concessions include such things as tax exemption on church property and the allowance of discrimination based on religion in hiring of people for employment by churches and church-related institutions. Unique constraints include not allowing religious institutions the use of tax funds for overtly sectarian purposes, such as disallowing tax funds for parochial schools while providing such funds for public schools.

The history of these various rulings is lengthy and complex. Decisions have been varied, contradictory, and inconsistent. This is not surprising. After all, the justices are only human and not infallible. Religious freedom and separation of church and state are new concepts on the stage of human history, and few precedents guide current decisions. Furthermore, the justices are often appointed for political reasons, and political parties wax and wane. Also, changes in society bring new situations calling for decisions related to church and state.

The justices have endeavored to discern the intent of the nation's founders in regard to the First Amendment. The basic tenor of the rulings of the Supreme Court has varied over time. Although it is an oversimplification, many authorities on the history of the United States Supreme Court indicate that two basic interpretations of the intent of the founders are represented in the decisions of the Court.

One is a strict separationist approach, often termed the "broad or no-aid view." Those who follow this line of interpretation believe that those who drafted the First Amendment intended it to apply broadly to the relation of religion and government. They intended it to prevent the government from endorsing and aiding religion in general, not just as a ban on establishing a national religion or preferring one religion over another.

The other approach is often referred to as the "narrow, equal treatment, or nonpreferentialist view." Those who advocate this interpretation insist that the founders intended only to prohibit the establishment of a national church or laws that preferred one religion over another. They would affirm government aid to religion generally and evenhandedly. In other words, they contend that the government can support religious activity as long as no single religion is preferred over another and no one is forced to support any religion.

The surviving documents from the Constitutional Convention and the states' ratification process leave room for interpretation as to what the founders intended. However, the separationist position appears more compatible with the prevailing opinions of the founders, especially in light of the fact that the equal treatment approach was considered and rejected by them in debate over the wording of the First Amendment.[17]

Very few decisions of the Court on church-state issues have been unanimous, and many have been decided by a single vote. Noonan comments, "No area of modern law, it may be boldly asserted, has been so marked by sectarian struggle, so strained by fundamental fissures, so reflective of deep American doubts and aspirations."[18] Any effort to summarize the complex array of decisions is subject to ridicule. Keeping that in mind, let's examine briefly how the United States Supreme Court has dealt with the two clauses of the First Amendment.

The Establishment Clause

Concerning the establishment clause, law professor Robert T. Miller notes, "The United States Supreme Court was not faced squarely with the necessity of construing the Amendment's 'establishment of reli-gion' clause until 1947."[19] At that time Justice Hugo Black, who wrote for the majority in the landmark case of *Everson v. Board of Education*, stated: "In the words of Jefferson, the clause against establishment of religion by laws was intended to erect a 'wall of separation between church and state.'"[20]

The Court has been called on to decide whether a number of practices result in an "establishment of religion" and are therefore unconstitutional. The cases related to the establishment clause tend to fall into two categories. One has to do with attempts by the govern-ment to promote religion, such as government-sponsored religious exercises in public schools. The other category has to do with cases where the government supports with tax funds institutions or pro-grams that are clearly religious.

Through the years the Court has developed various "tests" for determining the constitutionality of acts under the establishment clause. They include the Lemon Test, the Coercion Test, and the Endorsement Test. These have been applied in various ways and have been subject to criticism, revision, and interpretation.[21]

From 1947 until the late 1980s the Court adopted a fairly consis-tent approach that prohibited any level of government from funding religious activities. Most of the cases related to education. The Court basically did not approve funding that would benefit in a direct way religious schools and other organizations that were primarily reli-gious in nature. It did approve some so-called secular programs that benefited students, such as school lunch programs, secular textbooks, and school transportation.

The Court also ruled that certain religious activities carried out by government-supported entities, such as public schools, were not constitutional and violated the establishment clause. On this basis, for example, in the early 1960s the Court ruled that government-scripted and conducted prayers and Bible reading in public schools were unconstitutional.

Since the late 1980s the Court has moved more toward a nonpref-erentialist, equal treatment, or narrow approach. Although the Court has shifted its position in some ways, it has never indicated that the establishment of a national church is permitted or that direct payment to churches for religious activity is acceptable.

In close votes the Court has approved so-called *indirect* funding of religious activity. Some justices have contended that total division of religion and government is neither possible nor preferable, and that separation of church and state, while valid, is a matter of degree. Strict separationists view this trend of the Court as undesirable, an undermining of the establishment clause, and a potential serious threat to religious freedom.

In regard to the establishment clause, most proponents of both the broad and narrow view profess to want government neutrality toward religion. However, they often use the term *neutrality* differently. Those of the broad view use *neutrality* to mean that government usually must treat religion differently from secular activities. For example, public school teachers can teach and say many things in the classroom, but they are not to lead in prayer or worship. Those of the narrow view use neutrality to mean that government should treat religion the same as other matters. For example, if the government can provide tax funds for public schools it ought to be able to do the same for religious schools.

The Free Exercise Clause

The courts have dealt with a wide variety of activities related to the free exercise clause, such as snake handling in worship services; animal sacrifice as religious ritual; polygamy in marriage; religious solicitation in public places; conscientious objection to military service; chaplains in prisons and the military; blood transfusions for children of Jehovah's Witnesses; and the use of drugs in religious ceremonies.

Clearly the free exercise of religion is not absolute. As law professor Robert T. Miller observes, "As with all other liberties, freedom of religion is not without limits. . . .The guaranty of religious freedom is broad, but it does not follow that it is not subject to restraints in the interest of good order, morality, and the preservation of the welfare of the state."[22]

Thus the Court has been called on to determine the legitimate extent of free exercise. Groups and individuals are generally free to carry out whatever religious activities are in keeping with their convictions. However, this does not imply the right to act in ways that disturb public peace, create a public nuisance, endanger the health and well-being of themselves or of others, or seriously threaten public policy. Public demonstrations for religious purposes are freely allowed, but they are not to endanger people or disrupt normal operations of a community. The courts have ruled that reasonable regulations and ordinances related to public activity do not infringe on religious freedom.

The prevailing view of the Court in decisions rendered prior to 1990 was that the government should not interfere with the free exercise of religion unless it has a "compelling interest" to do so. The "compelling interest" concept is that government must show that a very important public health, safety, or welfare concern is threatened by a religious activity before it can be permitted to restrict that activity. Furthermore, the restraint on the religious practice must be by the least restrictive means available.

In 1990 a shift to what is often termed a "majoritarian attitude" took place. For example, in a 1990 case involving the use of peyote by Native Americans in worship, the Court ruled that the law making such practice illegal did not violate the religious freedom of the Native Americans. The Court reasoned that as long as a law is neutral and generally applied the religious claimant is not entitled to any heightened constitutional protection. This equal treatment approach decreed that a compelling interest protection for religious freedom was no longer an acceptable test, not just for Native Americans but for everyone.

The trend to restrict the free exercise of religion for other than very compelling reasons is considered dangerous by many people. Justice Sandra Day O'Conner wrote concerning this that the First Amendment was

enacted precisely to protect the rights of those whose religious practices are not shared by the majority and may be viewed with hostility. . . . The compelling interest test reflects the First Amendment's mandate of preserving religious liberty to the fullest extent possible in a pluralistic

society. For the Court to deem the command a "luxury" is to denigrate
"[t]he very purpose of a Bill of Rights."[23]

The Bill of Rights was not intended to protect the majority but the minorities. As Stokes and Pfeffer stated, "The free exercise clause has never meant that a majority could use the machinery of the State to practice its beliefs. Freedom of worship is not dependent upon the outcome of any election."[24] Justice Robert Jackson strongly emphasized this when he wrote, "The very purpose of a Bill of Rights was to withdraw certain subjects from the vicissitudes of political controversy, to place them beyond the reach of majorities and officials and to establish them as legal principles to be applied by the courts."[25]

The views of Justice O'Conner and Justice Jackson are compatible with those of James Madison, who introduced the First Amendment to Congress. In a letter to Thomas Jefferson in 1788, Madison explained why he favored a bill of rights. One of his reasons was that it might prevent the majority of the population from overriding the rights of the minority. He wrote,

In our Governments the real power lies in the majority of the Community, and the invasion of private rights is chiefly to be apprehended, not from acts of Government contrary to the sense of its constituents, but from acts in which the Government is the mere instrument of the major members of the constituents.[26]

Congress passed the Religious Freedom Restoration Act in 1993 in an effort to preserve the free exercise of freedom "to the fullest extent possible," but the United States Supreme Court ruled the act unconstitutional as applied to the states. Many states have passed their own version to provide increased protection of religious freedom by restoring the "compelling interest" concept.

Conclusion

Baptists and many other Americans cherish religious freedom and believe the friendly separation of church and state is necessary to preserve it. Our changing and complex society plus the pushes and pulls of political theory and activity call both for continuing interpretation and defense of religious freedom and its corollary the separation of church and state.

As cited at the beginning of this chapter, Baptist theologian Edgar Young Mullins writing in 1908 about the principle of separation of church and state observed, "There will of course remain a borderland where it will not always be clear how to discriminate and apply the principle correctly." In regard to this borderland, Justice Sandra Day O'Conner commented a century later, "Those who would renegotiate the boundaries between church and state must answer a difficult question: Why would we trade a system that has served us so well for one that has served others so poorly."[27]

CHAPTER *Six*

The Baptist Devotion to Religious Freedom

". . . It is impossible to define Baptists apart from their
devotion to the principle of complete religious freedom."

— WILLIAM R. ESTEP[1]
(1920–2000) Baptist historian,
Advocate for religious liberty

APTISTS HAVE ENDURED HARASSMENT, PUBLIC ridicule, economic loss,
political discrimination, arrest, imprisonment, torture, and
death because of their commitment to religious freedom. Through
it all, Baptists have steadfastly refused to abandon their goal of religious liberty for all people. Why?

The main reason for Baptist persistence is that the Baptist conviction about religious freedom is not some peripheral matter but is
central to Baptist belief. Baptists embrace the Scripture, "It is for freedom that Christ has set us free" (Galatians 5:1). The commitment to
full religious freedom for all is part of the *Baptist DNA*.

Religious Freedom: Bedrock of the Baptists

Every basic Baptist belief is not only based on the Bible but also relates in some way to religious freedom. Put another way, religious freedom is part of every core Baptist doctrine, polity, and practice. For a Baptist to recant belief in religious freedom is to subvert every other belief Baptists hold true about Christian faith and practice.

Baptists do not stake their devotion to religious freedom on any government document or philosophical teaching but on the word of God, the Bible, and its teachings concerning life, salvation, church, worship, and government. As church-state scholar Brent Walker has stated, "Baptists became champions of religious liberty and church-state separation in large measure because they are a people of the Book."[2]

Every group of Christians holds certain distinguishing beliefs. In religious terminology, *denomination* refers to such a collection of beliefs. Denominations are organized in a variety of ways. This is true of Baptists. Sometimes an organization of a denomination is thought of as the denomination itself, but it is not. It is an organizational expression of the denomination. Among Baptists in the United States, for example, the Progressive National Baptist Convention, the Southern Baptist Convention, and the Baptist General Convention of Texas are not separate denominations but different organizations within the Baptist denomination.

Although people within these various Baptist organizations may hold somewhat different interpretations of basic beliefs, they hold in common a commitment to these beliefs. Similarly, Baptist organizations may differ to some extent on exactly what religious freedom means and how it is to be applied. Nevertheless, Baptists of all stripes declare commitment to religious freedom. Too, each of the basic ingredients in the Baptist "recipe" of beliefs relates to this commitment to religious freedom.

The Baptist "Recipe"

What is the Baptist "recipe" of beliefs and practices? No *official* recipe exists because Baptists have no official creed or authoritative statement of faith. In fact, not all Baptists agree on what the difference is between a doctrine, a polity, or a practice. Even so, almost all Baptists agree that the Baptist "recipe" includes certain basic ingredients.

Basic doctrinal ingredients include: the lordship of Jesus Christ; the Bible as the sole written authority for faith and practice; salvation only by grace through faith in Jesus Christ as Lord and Savior; the competency of the individual soul; the priesthood of all believers; believer's baptism by immersion.

Basic polities include: a born-again, voluntary church membership; congregational governance with church leadership selected by the congregation; the independence of each church, with two ordinances, baptism and the Lord's Supper, as symbolic; voluntary cooperation.

Basic practices include: evangelism; missions; ministry to total human need; applying the gospel to the problems in society; Christian education.

The doctrines, polities, and practices of Baptists all relate to religious freedom. Understanding this relationship helps explain the tenacious, sacrificial commitment of Baptists to such freedom.

Bible-based doctrines of Baptists have been mentioned in previous chapters that dealt with the history of the Baptists' commitment to religious liberty. This chapter sets these doctrines forth more fully in their relationship to religious liberty. The next chapter explores the close relationship between religious liberty and Baptist polity and practices.

Religious Liberty and Basic Doctrines

At the opening session of the first World Congress of the Baptist World Alliance in 1905, the president of the Baptist World Alliance led the assembly of Baptists from many parts of the world in reciting the Apostles' Creed.[3] Baptists are not known as a creedal people. They often declare, *We have no creed but the Bible*. Why was a creed used in such a significant Baptist meeting?

Likely it was to acknowledge that Baptists form one part of the larger family of faith known as Christian. They hold in common with other denominations certain beliefs such as those contained in the Apostles' Creed.[4] Even so, although Baptists are part of the worldwide Christian movement, they cherish a cluster of doctrinal convictions that make them a distinct denomination. No single doctrine defines who Baptists are, but rather several interrelated beliefs bind Baptists together. Each of these relates to the Baptist conviction about religious freedom.

Religious Freedom and the Lordship of Christ

In a sermon preached in 1920 from the steps of the United States Capitol, Baptist pastor George W. Truett declared:

> *What are these fundamental Baptist principles which compel Baptists in Europe, in America, in some far-off seagirt island, to be forever contending for unrestricted religious liberty? First of all, and explaining all the rest, is the doctrine of the absolute Lordship of Jesus Christ. That doctrine is for Baptists the dominant fact in all their Christian experience, the nerve center of all their Christian life, the bedrock of all their church polity, the sheet anchor of all their hopes, the climax and crown of all their rejoicings.[5]*

The word *lord* has a number of meanings and definitions. For Baptists in relation to Jesus Christ, the word means that Jesus deserves total allegiance, loving service, and absolute obedience. Why? Because of who Jesus is and what Jesus has done.

Jesus is divine, one of the three persons of the Trinity: Father, Son, and Holy Spirit. Jesus declared, "I and the Father are one" (John 10:30). He said, "Anyone who has seen me has seen the Father" (John 14:9). He stated, "All authority in heaven and on earth has been given to me" (Matthew 28:18).

Jesus died on the cross for the sins of the world and as such is worthy of all praise and honor as Lord (Revelation 5:6–13). Jesus rose from the dead, indicating his power over death itself, a fact that led his disciple to exclaim, "My Lord and my God" (John 20:28). Jesus ascended into heaven and there makes intercession for us. He is coming again to bring a new heaven and new earth. With worshipful awe we declare, "Come, Lord Jesus (Rev. 22:20).

The extent of Christ's lordship knows no bounds. He is the Lord of all people (Philippians 2:10-11), the source of all creation (John 1:3), and Lord of churches (Matt. 16:18; Ephesians 1:22-23). Not everyone acknowledges Jesus' lordship, but the Christian life begins with the confession of Jesus as Lord (Romans 10:9).

Almost all Christian groups believe in the lordship of Jesus Christ in some way. Baptists believe that the lordship or authority of Jesus relates *directly* to his disciples and churches, not through some human authority. Baptists insist that Jesus did not delegate his authority to governmental rulers or church leaders: not to kings, parliaments, congresses, popes, bishops, pastors, conventions, committees, or any other entity.

Since Jesus is Lord, he is to be obeyed. Jesus said, "Why do you call me, Lord, Lord, and do not do what I say?" (Luke 6:46). Jesus commanded that we share the gospel to the ends of the earth and minister to the total needs of people. Religious freedom enhances the ability to do this.

The lordship of Christ means individuals and churches should be free from coercion by government or religious organizations in spiritual and religious matters. This conviction has cost Baptists dearly. Because Baptists have not and will not acknowledge the authority of governments in matters of faith, they have been condemned as traitors, anarchists, and seditionists. Because Baptists have not and will not bow to the decrees of powerful church groups, they have been condemned as heretics.

The accusations are false. However, the severe persecutions that the accusations have brought on Baptists are real. In spite of false accusations and severe persecution, Baptists have steadfastly championed full religious freedom for all people.

Religious Freedom and the Authority of the Bible

That the Bible is the sole written authority for Christian faith and practice is a cardinal Baptist belief. The word "written" is significant because God is the ultimate authority. The Bible is authoritative because it is from God, about God, and leads people to God (2 Timothy 3:15–17). Baptists emphasize the Bible as their "sole written authority" in contrast to some other religious groups who claim that certain writings are authoritative in addition to the Bible. Baptists reject the authority of such written statements and accept only the Bible.

Baptists contend the Bible's teachings form the basis for their doctrine, including belief in religious freedom. Baptist historian William Brackney declares, "For Baptists, the Bible is the sole font of revelation which speaks to both the intellect and the experience, the Church and the individual."[6]

No individual or group of people has authority over Baptists in regard to religious faith and practice—only the Bible. Thus Baptists claim freedom from any human authority and look only to the divine authority of the Bible as the word of God. That is why Thomas Helwys in his statement to King James about the limits of the king's authority regarding spiritual matters declared, "This is made evident to our lord the king by the Scriptures."[7]

The authority of the Bible is one reason Baptists champion religious freedom. People ought to be free to read the Bible, interpret the Bible, and follow the teachings of the Bible as they understand them. Of course, sound principles of biblical interpretation should be followed in the interpretation of Scripture, including reliance on the Holy Spirit for guidance.

The Baptist commitment to religious freedom calls for all people to have access to the Bible in their own language. Baptists therefore have condemned tyrannical secular governments as well as authoritarian religious groups for restricting the distribution of Bibles. Believing in the importance of the Bible, Baptists strive to get Bibles in the hands of people everywhere and to provide opportunities for the study of the Bible. Thankfully we have the freedom to do these things.

Baptists believe people ought to be free not only to possess and read the Bible but also to interpret it. A particular interpretation of the Bible should not be forced on people. Although Baptists do not believe every interpretation of the Bible is correct, most Baptists contend there is no human authority to dictate which one *is* correct. Therefore, in regard to interpreting the Bible, they advocate a free exchange of views while praying for the Holy Spirit's guidance.

Some would say biblical interpretation should be in the hands of *experts* or especially gifted or mature Christians. But who or what group has the authority to determine the identity of these *experts*? Furthermore, who has the authority to decide the person or persons to be in charge of determining who the *experts* are? Who or what group has authority to determine whether they have indeed provided a *correct* interpretation of the Bible?

Throughout history there have been those, even among Baptists, who have presumed to have *the* correct interpretation of Scripture and demanded all others believe as they did. However, most Baptists have resisted the temptation to conformity, preferring to live in the messiness of conflicting interpretations of Scripture that results from religious freedom than to surrender to the neatness of forced conformity without such freedom.

Therefore, Baptists hold to their view of the freedom of each Christian to interpret the Bible under the direction of the Holy Spirit, even while recognizing the human imperfections in such an approach. After all, since imperfect humans are interpreting the perfect word of God, the interpretations cannot be expected to be perfect, regardless of the process involved.

Responsible freedom in Christ demands freedom to study the Bible carefully. To avoid the pitfall of a purely individualistic interpretation of the Bible, Baptists encourage that interpretation be carried out within the framework of a worshiping community in which believers share freely with one another their insights. This approach calls for religious freedom, the freedom for believers to fellowship, assemble, and share with one another.

Baptists also believe people ought to be free to act in accordance with their interpretation of biblical teaching. As long as these actions do not harm or impinge on the freedom of others, neither government nor church authorities ought to interfere.

Clearly the Baptist approach to the Bible calls for religious liberty. Because of the sacrifice of a multitude of people, we enjoy religious

freedom that allows us to possess, study, and follow the Bible's teachings. Unfortunately many people possess Bibles but never use them.
What a terrible waste of the freedom multitudes suffered and died to
make possible!

Religious Freedom and Salvation by Grace through Faith Alone

The Bible teaches that all have sinned and that the penalty for sin is
eternal death. However, God by his grace has provided a way for sin to
be forgiven, hell avoided, and heaven gained. That way is faith in his
Son, Jesus Christ (Rom. 3:23; 6:23).

Salvation, according to the Bible, is solely by grace and faith, not
by works or any human effort (Eph. 2:8–9). Baptists do not deny the
importance of such things as baptism, church membership, and good
deeds, but they do deny that salvation is the result of any of these.

According to the Bible, a person who has experienced salvation
will want to be baptized, be a member of a church, participate in the
Lord's Supper, and do what is right and good. But these are the result
of salvation and not the cause of it. For example, the Bible indicates
that good works do not result in salvation, but salvation is to result
in good works (Eph. 2:10). People ought to be free to put into practice these results of their salvation.

Saving faith is an individual matter. No one can believe in Christ
in behalf of another for salvation. Salvation does not result from
being a member of a family of Christians or by being a citizen of a
nation that professes Christianity, but only by personal faith in Christ
as Savior and Lord.

On the basis of the Bible's teachings, Baptists believe true faith
cannot be coerced. Genuine faith is always voluntary. The ministry of
Jesus indicates the voluntary nature of faith in him. Although Jesus
clearly set forth the consequences of belief and unbelief, he never used
any sort of force when he urged people to believe in and to follow
him. The New Testament records that Jesus' disciples likewise presented faith as a voluntary response to the gospel.

Baptists have therefore consistently declared that people should
never be coerced into professing faith in Jesus. As Baptist preacher

George W. Truett observed, "Persecution may make men hypocrites, but it will not make them Christians."[8] Baptists have steadfastly advocated freedom of choice, that is, religious freedom.

Most Baptists believe in both the sovereignty of God and human freedom of choice. They acknowledge there seems to be no logical way to reconcile the two and that Scriptures can be cited in support of both of these viewpoints. As the Baptists who wrote the "Articles of Faith" for the Union Baptist Association in Texas in 1840 declared, "We believe in the doctrine of God's sovereignty, and man's free agency as an accountable being."[9]

Grace means that salvation is a gift from God. Like all gifts it must be accepted before becoming effectual. No person, religious organization, or government ought to stand in the way of a person responding by faith and receiving this gift from God. And since faith cannot be forced but must be exercised voluntarily, no entity should endeavor to coerce acceptance of God's grace gift of salvation in Christ. Baptists have a responsibility to insist constantly on religious freedom, the freedom to respond and the freedom from coercion to respond.

Religious Freedom and Soul Competency

Baptist theologian E. Y. Mullins in *The Axioms of Religion* stated that "the doctrine of the soul's competency in religion under God is the distinctive historical significance of the Baptists."[10] Further, Baptist historian H. Leon McBeth wrote, "The concept of the soul's competency is more than a single doctrine. Actually, it undergirds all the other doctrines of the faith."[11] Other notable Baptist leaders agree on the importance of this doctrine. For example, pastor-theologian Herschel Hobbs stated, "Out of this principle flow all other elements of Baptist belief. . . ."[12]

The Baptist belief that people have the God-given competence to make choices in regard to God's will is based on the Bible. Baptists hold dear the Bible's stories and teachings about such competence. They also acknowledge that the Bible teaches that God holds people accountable for their choices.

Under the umbrella of the term *soul competency* are found at least two major beliefs: (1) God gives people the ability or competence to know and respond to his will. This is a gift from God and not a human achievement. (2) People should be free from external restraint to exercise this competency. The second of these is often referred to as *liberty of conscience, soul freedom,* or *freedom of conscience.*

Jesus never violated the soul freedom of individuals. Furthermore, the leaders in the New Testament churches never tried to force anyone to follow Jesus as Lord and Savior. They modeled liberty of conscience. In fact, they resisted religious and governmental authorities who tried to force them not to speak publicly about Jesus (Acts 5:17–42).

Baptists have endeavored to follow the example of Jesus and of the New Testament churches in regard to liberty of conscience. When they have been true to their basic convictions, Baptists have avoided any coercion in regard to faith and practice, believing that individuals should be free to follow the dictates of their conscience. Furthermore, they have opposed attempts by both religious and government organizations to force people to affirm certain doctrines or to worship in particular ways.

Baptists believe soul competency calls for religious freedom for all. Liberty of conscience means no individual or group should attempt to force a person to believe or worship in ways that violate his or her conscience. This does not mean people ought not be urged to believe in Jesus as Lord and Savior or to follow the teachings of the Bible. Persuasion is acceptable; coercion is not.

Does soul competency mean an individual needs nothing other than his or her own personal sense of God's will? No. The responsible person will exercise liberty of conscience by seeking direction from the Bible, the Holy Spirit, and other followers of Christ. In our country we enjoy the freedom to do these and should utilize that freedom.

Could soul competency lead to spiritual anarchy, each person doing what is right in his or her own eyes? Perhaps, but Baptists believe also in the importance of the fellowship of believers that would curtail such anarchy. People should be humble enough to admit their inadequacies and seek the wisdom of the community of faith. Of course, the individual is still responsible for his or her decision. People ought to utilize religious freedom to participate fully in such a fellowship of faith.

The religious freedom we enjoy carries with it accountability. We have a responsibility to use our freedom to utilize our soul competency and to see that others are not thwarted in utilizing theirs.

Religious Freedom and the Priesthood of All Believers

Soul competency relates closely to another Bible teaching precious to Baptists: the priesthood of all believers. The Bible teaches that when people exercise their soul competency to believe voluntarily in Jesus as Lord and Savior, they become believer priests (1 Peter 2:9; Rev. 1:6; 5:10). If challenged as to their priestly authority to baptize and administer the Lord's Supper, Baptists declare, as did the Anabaptists, *We have our authority from the Bible, which teaches that all believers in Christ are priests.*

Being a priest provides both a marvelous opportunity and a serious responsibility. The opportunity is to go directly to God without the need of any intermediary (Hebrews 10:19–22). The responsibility is to serve God, share the knowledge of God through word and deed, and minister to other people.

Baptists insist that people ought to be free to exercise this marvelous opportunity and awesome responsibility. Neither ecclesiastical nor governmental entities should stand in the way of a person's functioning as a believer priest.

Each believer priest is to share the good news about Jesus with others and minister to the needs of people in Jesus' name. Therefore, believer priests should be free from government or church interference to share and minister in this fashion. Thus religious freedom is vital for the function of believer priests.

Furthermore, each believer priest should realize the importance of being part of a community of priests. In fact, the New Testament speaks of the priesthood of believers—*plural*. This expression indicates a fellowship or community of priests who worship together, learn from one another, and serve one another. Believer priests ought to be free to join voluntarily with others in this sort of fellowship, such as in a church or Bible study group, without government or religious organizations obstructing them. Religious freedom is necessary for believer priests to be all God intended them to be.

Possessing the religious freedom we enjoy in our country carries a responsibility to utilize it as believer priests. Among other things this means seeking fellowship with God through prayer and worship, confessing faith in Christ openly, being part of a community of fellow believer priests, and ministering to the total needs of people.

Religious Freedom and Believer's Baptism by Immersion

Baptists interpret the New Testament as indicating that baptism was always by immersion of the believer (Acts 8:26–39; Rom. 6:3–5; Colossians 2:12); followed conversion and never preceded it; and was not necessary for salvation (Acts 2:1–41; 8:36–39; 16:30–33). Baptists believe baptism should be administered only to those who have made a personal faith commitment to Jesus Christ as Lord and Savior.

The New Testament records that those who made a faith commitment to follow Jesus as Lord always did so voluntarily. Therefore, baptism as a symbol of such commitment was also voluntary. In the time of the New Testament, never was anyone forced to submit to baptism. Baptists believe that should be true for all times.

Because of these convictions based on the Bible, Baptists have never condoned baptisms forced on people by the power of governments and have refused to baptize infants. Baptists demonstrate love for babies in many ways, such as through child care institutions, adoption programs, and church educational activities, but they do not baptize babies. Why? Because baptism is for those who have put their faith in Christ as Savior and Lord, and babies are incapable of such faith. Furthermore, people who are baptized are to be baptized voluntarily, and infants are not able to make such a voluntary choice.

Baptists consider the baptism of infants as contrary to New Testament teaching. Therefore, when an adult who has been "baptized" as an infant makes a profession of faith in Christ, most Baptists believe the person should be encouraged to experience believer's baptism.

Both the refusal to baptize infants and the practice of baptizing adults who have been baptized as infants have brought much persecution to Baptists. For many centuries in Europe and in parts of America, to refuse to baptize infants and to baptize adults who had been baptized as infants was against the law. Such laws were one of the many negative results of the union of church and state. Baptists insisted that the government had no right to make such laws and continued to practice believer's baptism in spite of the persecution that resulted. Baptists also campaigned for full religious freedom so people could follow whatever convictions they held concerning baptism and other religious activities.

Baptists are one of the few denominations that practice believer's baptism by immersion as a symbol of having been saved and not as a necessity to be saved. Baptism is a public act of obedience to Jesus Christ as Lord. That is one reason Baptists refer to baptism as an *ordinance*; they believe Christ *ordered* it. In the United States, we are free to obey this command of Jesus publicly without fear of persecution. We should strive to make this opportunity possible in all countries.

Conclusion

Each of these basic beliefs is part of the Baptist "recipe." Too, each relates to religious freedom, helping to explain the zeal of Baptists for such freedom. Furthermore, these basic beliefs form the foundation for Baptist polity and practices, which also relate to religious liberty. That is the subject of the next chapter. Obviously there is no way to understand or to describe Baptists apart from their passion for religious liberty.

CHAPTER *Seven*

Religious Freedom and Baptist Polity and Practices

"This outward forcing men in the worship of
God, is the ready way to make men dissemblers
and hypocrites before God. . . ."

— JOHN CLARKE[1]
(1609–1676) Baptist physician
and pastor, Proponent of
religious freedom

RELIGIOUS LIBERTY STRENGTHENS THE BAPTIST effort to serve all people in the name of Christ. Lack of freedom handicaps these efforts. Baptist church governance and organization as well as mission and ministry all relate to religious freedom.

Religious Freedom and Polity

Polity describes the organization, function, and governance of religious groups, including Baptists. Bible-based Baptist polities, such as a born-again church membership, congregational governance, church independence, and voluntary cooperation, function best where there is religious freedom.

Religious Freedom and a Born-Again Church Membership

Baptists use various terms to describe their concept of church, such as *regenerate church, gathered church, voluntary church, born-again church,* and *believers' church.* Whatever term is used, Baptists agree on the basic meaning: a church is a fellowship of people who have followed Jesus as Lord voluntarily, experienced believer's baptism voluntarily, and associated with one another voluntarily under Jesus' lordship and the guidance of the Holy Spirit for worship, Christian nurture, and ministry.

Baptists most frequently use the word *church* to refer to a local congregation of baptized believers, as the Bible does. However, Baptists acknowledge that the New Testament "speaks also of the church as the body of Christ which includes all of the redeemed of all the ages."[2]

Baptists have always opposed government requirements that people be members of and/or attend official government-supported churches. They advocate that people should be free to choose whatever fellowship of Christians the Holy Spirit leads them to be part of and to worship according to the dictate of their conscience.

People should be neither forced nor forbidden to be a member of any church. As we have seen, for expressing this conviction and choosing to worship apart from the official state church, Baptists in the past were severely persecuted. Why did Baptists maintain this view in spite of fierce opposition? Because the Bible, not human laws regarding spiritual matters, guides Baptists in their views of the nature of church and worship.

Baptists interpret the Bible to teach that only people who have been born again should be members of a church. This new birth does not come by merely reciting facts about Jesus but by a genuine voluntary experience of faith in Jesus as Lord and Savior (John 1:12–13; 3:1–21).

The New Testament affirms this concept of church (see Acts 2:47; 1 Corinthians 1:2; 12:12–31). Although the ideal of a church made up only of born-again people may never have been realized fully even in

New Testament times, this ideal has always remained the standard for Baptists. To force people to be part of a particular church or to worship in a specific way subverts this ideal.

Baptists believe not only that *only* born-again people ought to be baptized and become members of a church but also that born-again people *should* want to be baptized and become members of a church. Therefore, Baptists have condemned the laws of governments and/or the policies of religious groups that either prohibit or restrict people from being baptized and becoming a member of a church of their choice.

Baptists also oppose the laws of governments that make only one religion legal and ban all others, thus restricting freedom of choice. Too, they condemn the actions of religious groups that persecute people who choose not to be part of that group. In addition, they believe people ought to be free to start new churches without seeking permission from any ecclesiastical or government authorities.[3]

This freedom extends beyond simply starting or joining a church. People should be free to take part in all parts of the life of a church, including worship, Bible study, discipleship classes, evangelistic outreach, and ministry. No entity should stand in the way of Christians "meeting together" (Hebrews 10:25).

Baptists have insisted on and worked for full religious freedom for all people as one means of helping develop the New Testament ideal for churches. Of course, religious freedom is not essential for regenerate church membership. Such membership has existed even when laws have been contrary to it. People have met and worshiped in secrecy, in so-called underground churches, and still do, aware of the terrible consequences if discovered.

Such conditions are far from ideal. Voluntary church membership can function best where there is religious freedom, where people are not forced to be part of a particular religious group or forcefully prohibited from being part of a group of their choice.

Religious Freedom and Congregational Church Governance

The Bible teaches that only Jesus is to be Head or Ruler of the church. Jesus said, "I will build my church" (Matthew 16:18). The earliest churches recognized Christ as the Head of the church (Ephesians 4:15; Philippians 2:11). He is the Head and the members are his body. Thus the believer priests who comprise a church, while equal, are all under the lordship of Christ. Through prayer, meditation, and discussion, they are to seek Christ's will for the church, not theirs.

On the basis of the Bible, Baptists insist that Jesus delegated his lordship to no one. He alone is Lord. No one carries his authority. Therefore, each member of the body of Christ ought to have an opportunity and responsibility to exercise his or her competency as a believer priest to find the will of Christ as decisions are made for the church. Baptists believe this is the model for church governance set forth in the Bible (Acts 6:1–6; 13: 1–3; 15:22; 2 Corinthians 8:1–13).[4]

Such church governance functions best where religious freedom prevails, both within the membership and outside of it. The believer priests in the church ought to be free from external control by governmental or religious authorities.

Church members ought also to be free from control from any person or group within the church. Pastors, deacons, and other people are to be selected by the congregation to provide leadership, but such people should exercise servanthood and not dictatorship (1 Peter 5:1–5).

The members may choose to delegate responsibilities to certain individuals or groups within the church membership, but the ultimate authority remains with the total body. For example, a church may select a committee to search for and recommend a pastor for the church, but the decision about the final selection of the pastor rests with the entire church.

Baptists believe Christ gave to congregations of believers two ordinances: baptism and the Lord's Supper. They are termed *ordinances* because Jesus ordered his followers to observe them. Each is symbolic in the sense that while both are important, neither is necessary for salvation. Baptists contend that religious freedom should be exercised in regard to these ordinances. No governmental or ecclesiastical authority should dictate matters related to them. The Bible is the guide for the ordinances, and people should be free to follow the Bible's teachings about them.

Religious Freedom and Church Independence

The independence of churches relates closely to congregational governance. In fact, without independence there could be no true congregational governance. A Baptist church is to govern itself without any outside human direction or control.

Certainly Baptist churches do not claim to be absolutely independent or autonomous. They recognize the ultimate authority of Jesus as Lord of the church. When autonomy is interpreted to mean that individuals or churches are free to do as *they* please, the results are negative. Always the lordship of Christ ought to be kept central. Churches are free to *do as Christ pleases.*

Baptist denominational organizations, such as associations and conventions, have no authority over a Baptist church. For any of these organizations to attempt to control an individual church is to violate a basic Baptist conviction about freedom in church polity. Being autonomous, each local congregation determines, among other things, its form of worship, selects its pastoral leadership, decides how tithes and offerings are to be used, and directs other church-related affairs without outside control or supervision.

Not only are Baptist churches independent of any denominational control, but they also insist they are to be free of any government effort to dictate spiritual matters. Certainly they heed the Bible's instruction to be law-abiding and to honor government officials, but they have consistently refused to recognize any government authority regarding spiritual matters.

Why have Baptists held so steadfastly to the independence of local congregations when the conviction has cost them terrible persecution? Baptists believe that no other pattern of church relationships is in keeping with the teachings of the Bible, the authority for faith and practice.

The Bible sets forth church autonomy as the pattern for New Testament churches. Each congregation of believers was independent under the lordship of Christ. They related to each other in fellowship, but no human individual or group exercised authority over a congregation. For example, each of the seven churches in Asia Minor to which the Revelation was directed existed as a separate entity, under no authority except that of Jesus Christ. The risen and glorified Christ gave direction to the churches through the revelation given to John (Revelation 1–3).

Furthermore, the New Testament churches selected from their own membership people to care for the physical needs of members (Acts 6:3-6), determined who would be commissioned for specific ministries (Acts 13:1-3), and disciplined their own members (Matt. 18:15-17; 1 Cor. 5:1-13). These actions were taken under the lordship of Christ and the guidance of the Holy Spirit without any external direction or control. Leaders such as the Apostle Paul relied on persuasion and example rather than dictatorial demands when writing to the churches about issues and practices.

The Bible also indicates that the churches in the New Testament resisted the efforts of governmental and religious authorities to dictate religious belief and practice, declaring that they must obey God, not human beings (Acts 4:18-20; 5:29). Such autonomy finds its finest expression where there is religious freedom.

Church independence functions best where there is religious freedom, where no ecclesiastical or government authorities attempt to dictate to a church. We have this freedom in the United States. Freedom always carries an awesome responsibility. One aspect of that responsibility is to resist any effort to interfere with the spiritual function of a church by any outside human entity.

Religious Freedom and Voluntary Cooperation

The Bible indicates that churches are to be involved in evangelism, missions, and ministry to human need in Jesus' name. An individual church, regardless of how large it might be, cannot possibly fulfill this biblical mandate.

Therefore, early Baptists faced a major dilemma: How could independent congregations fulfill the command of Christ to take the gospel to the entire world without forming some sort of connection among churches that possibly could undermine their freedom and autonomy?

Finally Baptists, led by the Holy Spirit, realized they could be faithful in their commitment to church independence and also fulfill the other expectations the Lord has for his churches. How? Through voluntary cooperation of churches!

The New Testament records examples of such cooperation, indicating that was the Lord's plan for his churches. In these earliest churches, voluntary cooperation was for the sake of effective ministry to human need, for fellowship, and for missions and evangelism.

For example, the Apostle Paul wrote to the church in Corinth appealing for them to join with other churches in a voluntary collection to help meet the needs of Christians in Jerusalem. Paul made clear that the offering was to be voluntary. He did not command them to take the offering. No coercion was involved (2 Cor. 8:1—9:15). Another example of voluntary cooperation in the New Testament relates to evangelism and missions. A voluntary agreement was made that certain evangelists and missionaries would major on different people groups (Galatians 2:1–10).

Through the years Baptists have formed many organizations and institutions to enhance voluntary cooperation. Each of these is to be free of governmental control in spiritual matters. None of these is to have any authority over local churches.

Churches are free to relate or not to relate to one or more of these organizations. Thus Baptists are able to fulfill the Bible's mandate for ministry without violating the biblical teaching about church autonomy. Freedom can be maintained if all entities involved understand and are committed to this Bible-based polity.

With the understanding of the model for cooperation set forth in the Bible, Baptists were willing to launch efforts of cooperation. The voluntary aspect of these efforts was not difficult for Baptists. Voluntarism and freedom form a theme that permeates the Baptist symphony of beliefs and polities. What was lacking for many years among Baptists was not voluntarism but cooperation. With the Bible's example, Baptists embraced voluntary cooperation.

For cooperation to be truly voluntary, there must be no coercion from either government authorities or denominational entities. Efforts to force cooperation run counter to Baptist beliefs based on the Bible. Baptists ought to resist any attempts to mandate conformity. The commitment to and need for religious freedom demand such resistance.

Religious Freedom and Baptist Practices

Baptists emphasize practices such as evangelism, missions, ministry to total human need, action for social justice, and education. All of these are based on basic biblical doctrines and polities. *And each relates to religious freedom.*

The Bible says, "Do not use your freedom to indulge the sinful nature; rather, serve one another in love" (Gal. 5:13). Baptists endeavor to follow this biblical directive. As William Estep stated about Baptists in the past, ". . . Religious freedom was never an end in itself. It was simply the means by which the gospel could be freely proclaimed, responded to, and acted on without interference from an established church or an all-encompassing state."[5] Such should be the case with Baptists today.

Religious Freedom and Evangelism

The Baptist commitment to evangelism rests solidly on basic Bible teachings. Because Jesus is Lord, those who follow him are to do as he directs. In what is often termed the Great Commission, Jesus instructs his followers, "Therefore go and make disciples of all nations, baptizing them in the name of the Father and of the Son and of the Holy Spirit" (Matt. 28:19). Furthermore, Jesus declared, "You will be my witnesses" (Acts 1:8). In what is sometimes referred to as the Great Commandment (Matt. 22:36–40), Jesus calls his disciples to love God and neighbor as self. Love of neighbor certainly calls for sharing the good news about Jesus with other people.

The Bible emphasizes that evangelism is important because salvation from eternal death to eternal life comes only through faith in God's grace gift of his Son, the Lord Jesus Christ (John 3:16–18; Eph. 2:8–10). The Bible records Jesus' teaching, "I am the way and the truth and the life. No one comes to the Father except through me" (John 14:6).

Since salvation comes only by a faith response to Jesus as Lord and Savior, the gospel ought to be shared so that people might know to believe in Jesus and be saved (Romans 10:13–17). Therefore, those who have found Christ as Lord have a responsibility to share the way to salvation with everyone everywhere in order that everyone might have opportunity to respond.

One of the major obstacles in our world to evangelism has been and continues to be lack of religious freedom. As preceding chapters have indicated, for many years laws in Europe and America made it illegal for Baptist individuals, churches, and other organizations to evangelize. Baptists believed so fervently in the responsibility to share the gospel that they continued to evangelize. Consequently, they were arrested, fined, imprisoned, and threatened with beatings and death.

Persecution not only hindered Baptists in sharing their faith but also caused people to hesitate to respond to the sharing of the gospel because they feared the consequences. However, numerous people risked the wrath of the government and the official church by making public professions of faith and being baptized.

By the late 1700s and early 1800s most of the laws against evangelism by Baptists and others had been eliminated in England and the United States. Baptists took the opportunity of this freedom to proclaim the gospel and start many new churches.

Today, though, in various parts of the world lack of religious freedom continues to hinder evangelism. In some countries, the government, often in alliance with the dominant religious group, makes it illegal for Baptists to start churches or share the gospel. In other countries, where the government is basically hostile to all religions, such as in Communist nations, severe restrictions exist for sharing the gospel openly and starting churches. Even in countries where the government professes neutrality and freedom of religion, people who are part of the dominant religious group often harass and even attack Baptists and others who attempt to share the gospel and to start churches.

The religious liberty in our country provides an opportunity and responsibility to evangelize. Such liberty does not exist everywhere in the world. Wherever people are prohibited either by law or public harassment from freely proclaiming and voluntarily responding to the gospel, Baptists of today ought to be in the forefront advocating religious liberty for everyone.

Religious Freedom and Missions

Jesus commanded that the gospel be taken to all people everywhere (Matt. 28:18–20; John 20:21; Acts 1:8). The Bible is a missionary book. From its beginning in Genesis (12:1–3) to its conclusion in Revelation (5:9; 7:9) the Bible sets forth God's desire that all the people of the world know him and his salvation. The Bible indicates that sharing the good news of Jesus calls for Christians to be sent to spread the word of salvation (Rom. 10:8–15). They go in the power of the Holy Spirit (Acts 1:8) with a desire for people to profess Jesus as Lord (John 3:16; Rom. 10:13).

Since missions entails evangelism, the comments about evangelism and religious freedom in the previous section of this chapter apply also to missions. There are differences in emphases and methods, however, between evangelism and missions. The emphasis in missions is on being sent, or going, to a place or culture different from one's home base.

Religious freedom becomes a major issue for missions when people go to share the gospel in a place where doing so is prohibited by law. This was the case with the first Baptist missionaries from the United States, Ann and Adoniram Judson. When they entered Burma in the early 1800s, the government opposed religious freedom and thwarted their missionary efforts. During war between Burma and England, Adoniram was imprisoned, and Ann ruined her health ministering to his needs in the horrible conditions of the prison. Religious freedom is still lacking in many places, and Christians continue to suffer as they carry out the missionary mandate.

The development of religious liberty in our country provided opportunity for missionary endeavor, and a sense of responsibility by

Baptists for missions enabled these endeavors to be carried out. Today the freedom continues to exist to garner support for missions and to send missionaries, both long-term career missionaries and short-term volunteers. We are accountable for this freedom. Our hope must be that Baptists will continue to utilize the freedom to share the gospel with people everywhere in the world.

However, not every place in the world is open for missionary activity. In a number of countries religious freedom does not exist. There Baptists and others are not free to share the gospel openly, disciple converts, and establish churches. Baptists have a responsibility to strive for all people everywhere to have the freedom to hear and respond to the gospel.

Religious Freedom and Ministry to Total Human Need

Ministry to meet total human need—physical, emotional, mental, social, as well as spiritual—is rooted in Baptist beliefs and polity based on the Bible. Each of these ministries relates to religious freedom.

Jesus as Lord taught the importance of ministry by his disciples. Jesus declared, "By this all men will know that you are my disciples, if you love one another" (John 13:35). When asked what the great commandment of the law was, Jesus answered that it was twofold: love for God and love for neighbor as self (Matt. 22:37-40). Love for neighbor, Jesus taught, is not mere emotion but acts of mercy meeting need (Luke 10:25-37). Jesus declared that a basis for eternal judgment is how well each person has met the needs of others (Matt. 25:31-46). Jesus set an example in his ministry of caring for all people and for their total need, and he commands his disciples to follow his example.

The Bible clearly teaches the importance of ministry to total human need. For example, the Bible declares that we are to love not just with words but with deeds of compassion (1 John 3:17-18). The New Testament churches did that, setting an example for all churches in the centuries to follow. The Bible also teaches that while we are not saved by good works but by faith, our salvation is to result in good works (Eph. 2:10). "Faith without deeds is useless," the Bible says (James 2:20).

The Bible states that those who are saved by faith in Jesus Christ as Lord and Savior become believer priests (1 Pet. 2:5; Rev. 1:6). Each believer priest has a responsibility to minister to others. In addition to ministry by individuals, Baptists have formed an array of organizations and institutions to meet need in Christ's name. These ministries are for the needs of all kinds of people in a wide variety of places.

Religious freedom plays a vital role in Baptist ministry to human need. Governments ought not stand in the way of ministry efforts. Individuals and churches should be free to choose which ministries to conduct apart from coercion by either government or religious authorities.

Baptist organizations often cooperate with government entities in ministry but strictly on a voluntary basis. Increasingly governments have entered the field of welfare and care of human need. The entanglement of government with religious ministry agencies raises questions related to church-state separation. Baptists believe the total person ought to receive ministry. It is not enough to care for the physical needs without also caring for the spiritual. If tax money is used to help support Baptist ministries, then the government may feel it needs to limit or eliminate distinctive Christian witness in these ministries. Therefore, the freer the ministry entities can remain from government support, the freer they are to share the gospel with those to whom ministry is given.

Baptists support ministries by freewill offerings, following the example set in the New Testament (2 Cor. 8:1–8). Funds collected for ministry either by taxation or denominational assessment would involve coercion and subvert freedom. Baptist ministry is rooted in voluntary participation, support, and cooperation. Therefore, Baptists have a responsibility to provide adequate support for ministries, both in financial contribution and in volunteer labor. Religious liberty in America enhances the ability to provide such support.

Religious Freedom and Applying the Gospel to Problems in Society

The world-renowned Baptist evangelist Billy Graham declared, "We as Christians have two responsibilities. One, to proclaim the Gospel of Jesus Christ as the only answer to man's deepest needs. Two, to apply as best we can the principles of Christianity to the social conditions around us."[6] Evangelism, ministry, and social action go hand in hand. Each is part of carrying out the Christian mission.

The application of the principles of Christianity calls for both ministry and social action. Ministry endeavors to heal a hurt. Social action strives to prevent the hurt. Admittedly, Baptists have been more involved in ministry than in social action, but Baptists have endeavored to right wrongs in our world. These actions are based on the bedrock of Baptist beliefs and relate directly to the importance of religious freedom.

The lordship of Christ calls for efforts to bring about a social order characterized by love and justice. Jesus is Lord of all (John 1:3; Phil. 2:9–11). He declared that his disciples should not only profess that he is Lord (John 13:13) but also act in accord with his lordship (Luke 6:46). The Lord of all desires that we do as he teaches and follow his example (Matt. 7:21–27).

Jesus initially announced his ministry publicly in terms that indicate his concern for all aspects of life (Luke 4:18–19). The teachings of Jesus address specific issues related to institutions of society, such as family and government (Matt. 19:3–12; 22:15–22). Jesus set an example of sacrificial service to benefit others and commanded his disciples to take up the cross and follow him (Matt. 16:24).

The Bible sets forth God's standards for all aspects of life—individuals, families, churches, economies, and governments—and calls for people to strive to meet these standards. God's will is for a just, humane, and moral social order, including religious freedom.

The New Testament sets forth God's standard for governments to function for the good of citizens (Rom. 13:1–7). Christian leaders declared the equality of everyone in Christ in a time when women and slaves were considered inferior (Gal. 3:28). New Testament writers condemned the usual pattern in society of pandering to the rich and ignoring the poor (James 2:1–9).

Baptists have used a number of methods to apply the gospel to all of life. Some of these have focused on strengthening the basic institutions of society. Others have majored on correcting wrongs in society.

Religious freedom figures into the Baptist efforts to apply the gospel to social conditions. Baptists believe that they, and all other people, ought to be free to express their convictions on social issues and to work to correct problems in society.

Unfortunately, Baptists have not always been in the forefront of struggles for justice and improved conditions for all. For various reasons, Baptists have all too often been guilty of ignoring social injustice. Too, Baptists have not always been on the correct side of social controversy, such as when many Baptists defended slavery and racial segregation. Fortunately, Baptists have come to condemn such practices.

Baptists have been major advocates for the application of the gospel to social conditions. Such advocates include Walter Rauschenbusch (1861–1918) and T. B. Maston (1897–1988). Among the significant contributions Baptists have made in the area of social change is one that relates to religious freedom itself. Baptists have been in the forefront of the effort to bring about religious freedom and its corollary the separation of church and state. The Baptist struggle for religious freedom has been for all people, not just for Baptists. One of the hallmarks of Baptist social action has been to work not just for the interests of Baptists but of everyone.

Religious freedom, along with freedom of speech, assembly, and the press, enables Baptists in America to be active participants in efforts for social reform. Such freedom carries the responsibility to take part in efforts to bring about change.

Religious Freedom and Christ-centered Education

Another major emphasis of Baptists is Christ-centered education. As with other emphases, this emphasis also relates directly to religious freedom.

The Baptist commitment to education comes from basic beliefs and polities. The lordship of Christ indicates the importance of learning. Jesus said, "Love the Lord your God with all your heart and with all your soul and with all your mind" (Matt. 22:37). He himself in his earthly ministry was a teacher. By his example Jesus emphasized the importance of teaching.

The Baptist devotion to the authority of the Bible calls for people to be able to read and understand the Bible. Education helps to make that possible. The Bible stresses the importance of enriching the mind as well as the spirit. Proverbs warns that "fools despise wisdom and discipline" (Proverbs 1:7). Since God is the Creator and Sustainer of everything (Genesis 1:1; Colossians 1:16), Christian education appropriately includes study of more than just spiritual matters.

Christian education can enhance the ministry of believer priests. Soul competency is a gift from God and not a human achievement; however, the competency to know and follow God's will is enriched by Christian education.

Congregational governance and church autonomy, two cardinal Baptist polities, can be strengthened by Christian education. A thorough knowledge of Baptist beliefs and practices helps church members carry out their governance opportunities and responsibilities more effectively.

Evangelism, missions, ministry, and the application of the gospel to all of life are all made more effective by Christian education. Such education helps to enhance the skills and knowledge needed for people to carry these out successfully.

Because of the importance of education, Baptists have fostered many different kinds of education. They have provided schools of various types for people to receive a formal education. In addition, they have made resources available for individuals to gain an informal, often self-taught, education. Many Baptists who lack high levels of formal education are well-educated, having utilized the many resources at their disposal. In addition, churches and other Baptist entities also deliver Christian education in many ways.

Religious freedom relates to Christian education in several ways. Such education helps people to be aware of the biblical, theological, and historical bases for such freedom and thus be better equipped to protect and preserve it.

Religious freedom enables Christian education to flourish. Where religious freedom is lacking, people are denied access to all of the resources of such education. People ought to be free to study the Bible and other materials without fear of persecution. People should be free to attend the school of their choice, to learn from teachers of their choice, and to have access to informational materials of their choice. Baptists have a responsibility to strive to make religious freedom a reality, to open the avenues to Christian learning for all people.

Education is a complex, controversial, and even divisive issue on many counts. No one should endeavor to oversimplify the issues, such as the nature of academic freedom in a church-related school and the pressures by some to gain tax support for such schools. However, Baptists have a responsibility to champion the cause of religious freedom and separation of church and state while facing honestly the challenges of dealing with specific issues and cases.

Conclusion

Each of the Bible-based doctrines and practices common to Baptists highlights the importance of religious freedom. Certainly these can be held and conducted where there is no freedom of religion. Baptists have done so through the centuries and suffered persecution as a result. However, each can best be expressed when "the freedom road" exists.

CHAPTER *Eight*

Religious Freedom: A Serious Responsibility

"If eternal vigilance is the price of freedom, it is especially true of religious liberty."

— HERSCHEL H. HOBBS[1]
(1907–1995) Baptist pastor
and theologian, Supporter of
religious liberty

WALK "THE FREEDOM ROAD." LISTEN to the cries of those burned alive, drowned, hanged, tortured in sadistic ways, torn apart on the rack, and imprisoned in squalor for the cause of religious freedom. Hear the pleas to princes and popes made by people for freedom of worship—pleas met with ridicule, silence, threat, and persecution. See the charred remains of books, pamphlets, and petitions that made the case for freedom and were burned by those in power.

Religious freedom is not free. No freedom is. The cost is always terribly high. Jesus paid with his life in cruel crucifixion so the greatest freedom of all would be available to us—freedom from the penalty and power of sin (Romans 5:6–21; 1 Peter 2:24.). Millions of courageous men and women have sacrificed life and health on battlefields so that in the United States we might enjoy the freedoms promised in the First Amendment to the Constitution.

Freedom—including religious freedom—is precious indeed! We should never take it for granted or utilize it without appreciation for those who have made it possible.

Protect Religious Freedom

Freedom is also fragile. What generations of people in the past paid for with their blood we can lose through our neglect.

Being fragile, freedom requires vigilant protection and appropriate use. We have been granted the gift of freedom. Now it is up to us to use it responsibly and to protect it diligently.

Threats to Religious Freedom

The danger of losing religious freedom always exists. Some people believe they have found the absolute truth about God and endeavor to force other people to believe as they do. Others desire an atheistic culture and would stamp out any freedom of religion. Still others are quite content to let other people dictate to them what to believe. Too, some people simply enjoy power and want to control others.

Religious freedom can be lost in many ways. Threats exist to the freedom we enjoy. Some of these threats are more dangerous than others, and some are only vague possibilities. All of these threats, though, are worth taking seriously.

A threat to religious freedom in the United States—one that seems almost too farfetched to consider—is *conquest by an outside enemy.* If our nation is conquered by powers that do not believe in religious freedom, then it will be denied us. Throughout history great nations and societies have felt immune to conquest only to fall to forces they had thought would never overpower them.

On the other hand, *the danger could come from within our country*. If a significant part of the population came to accept a form of government that denied religious freedom, we would lose our freedom of religion. Such a change in government could come through violent revolution or through political maneuvering. At the present time, that seems highly unlikely. The possibility exists, though, for the right combination of energy on the part of some and apathy on the part of others to form a potent mix for change that would result in loss of freedom.

Too, some people in our country advocate a total, absolute separation of religion and government, or an unfriendly separation of church and state, or even an atheistic state. Such views also are a potential threat to religious freedom.

A major threat to religious freedom is ignorance of the past and of the reasons we have such freedom in our nation. Many people believe that religious freedom has always existed in the United States as part of our culture, our ethos, our American *DNA*. It has not. As previous chapters have indicated, bringing religious freedom for all people was accomplished only after a long, bitter, bloody struggle.

Unfortunately, a multitude of Americans seem to possess neither knowledge of nor interest in the heritage that made religious liberty a reality. Such ignorance and apathy are dangerous. Those who do not know history are indeed liable to repeat it, as the familiar saying states. To repeat much of the past in regard to church-state relations would be horrible indeed.

Religious Freedom and Separation of Church and State

Baptists and the leading founders of our nation agreed that religious liberty is best—and perhaps *only*—achieved through strict but friendly separation of church and state. Therefore, opposition to this approach to separation of church and state, however well-intended, could lead to diminished religious freedom.

For Baptists, for whom religious freedom is vitally important to basic beliefs and practices, such an erosion of freedom would be especially tragic. Therefore, an awareness of the dangers to separation of church and state should be of special concern to Baptists.

Opposition to Separation of Church and State

In regard to church-state relations, Baptists have generally advocated friendly separation of church and state as the best means of providing religious freedom. Vast amounts of evidence indicate that the drafters of the Constitution of the United States and the First Amendment intended this concept of church-state relations to be the law of the land. However, from the origin of our nation to the current time, opposition to separation has existed.

Early Opposition

For many centuries the governments and government-supported churches in Europe violently rejected the concepts of religious freedom and church-state separation. In the United States, opposition to religious freedom and its corollary the separation of church and state existed from the time of the arrival of the first settlers from Europe. Many people sincerely believed separation of church and state would result in anarchy and a total breakdown of society.

Continuing Forms of Opposition

With the ratification of the Constitution and the First Amendment, the separation of church and state became a reality. For many years after ratification, general but not total acceptance of church-state separation existed. Separation always had its enemies. In recent years the attacks on separation have become more severe, due in part to changes in American society described in chapter five.

The attacks come from many sources. Separation of church and state has been termed "a deception of Satan."[2] A book by a law professor claims separation of church and state developed as an expression of anti-Catholic sentiment.[3] United States Supreme Court Chief Justice William Rehnquist wrote, "The 'wall of separation between church and state' is a metaphor based on bad history. . . ."[4] The pastor of a large Baptist church stated, "I believe this notion of the separation of church and state was the figment of some infidel's imagination."[5]

The claim is made that separation has caused secular humanism to become the "established" religion of the nation.[6]

Clearly separation of church and state is under siege. To neatly classify, define, or describe the various oppositions is not possible. Each position has within it many variations. Yet a brief general overview of the opposition to strict, friendly separation of church and state from professing Christians, painted with broad strokes, may provide insight into the challenges that exist.

The Total Union Approach to Church-State Relations

Some people advocate a union of church and state, of religion and government. *Reconstructionism*, sometimes termed *Dominion Theology*, represents perhaps the most extensive and extreme expression of this position.

Reconstructionism advocates a society in which the Bible in general and the law of the Old Testament in particular would be the law of the land. A major proponent of this position states, "Since there is only one true God, and His law is the expression of His unchanging nature and righteousness, then to abandon the Biblical law for another law-system is to change gods."[7]

Calvin's Geneva and the theocracy of the Massachusetts Bay Puritans are sometimes presented as societies where the Bible was the basis of the law. However, even Calvin's Geneva did not fully comply with the ideals of one of the leading Reconstructionists, who wrote, "Calvin wanted the establishment of the Christian religion; he could not have it, or could it last long in Geneva, without Biblical law."[8]

Christian Reconstructionism would totally obliterate separation of church and state. Although the followers of this view are few, the concept has an influence. "The Reconstructionists cannot be dismissed as a passing, and therefore irrelevant, side-current on the course of evangelical thought," according to careful students of the movement.[9] For example, some people seem to believe, as Reconstructionists advocate, that the Bible should, in a sense, indeed be the law of the land.

Baptists have consistently opposed union of church and state. While reverencing the Bible, they have not advocated its being the official law of a government. The Founding Fathers of the United States also opposed such a view, although they were familiar with the Bible and often quoted from it.

The Christian Nation Approach to Church-State Relations

The majority of Americans say they believe in God. The Christian religion has by far the most members of any religious group in the United States. Various Christian expressions and values exist in American life. The people who have shaped the nation's history have for the most part been professing Christians. Perhaps these are some of the reasons the United States is often referred to as a Christian nation. However, the Christian religion is not, and never has been, the official religion of the nation.

Church-state historian James E. Wood Jr. wrote, "From the time of the Puritans down to the present America's theocrats have contended against the principle of separation, *viz*, the secular state, and have sought through various means to have America declared a 'Christian nation'"[10] The definition of exactly what is meant by a "Christian nation" differs among its advocates.

Some proponents seem to relate the concept of a "Christian nation" to cultural consensus and the historical background of the founders. As one advocate of this view suggests, "America is often labelled 'a Christian nation' not because it was founded as such, but because its Founding Fathers were either Christians or had been influenced throughout their entire lives by the Christian consensus that surrounded them."[11] Some seem to want Christian values to be the official basis of the American legal system: "Our Founders never envisioned that the First Amendment would become a weapon to excise Christian or traditional religious expressions from the public arena."[12]

Others want the nation to be recognized officially as Christian. People who advocate the "Christian nation" approach quote from numerous sources in our nation's history to support their point of view, such as the Declaration of Independence.[13] However, the Declaration of Independence, as inspiring and significant as it is, is theistic and not distinctively Christian. Further, it "is not judicially enforceable, and it establishes no legal rights or duties."[14] The Constitution is the official judicial authority for the nation, and it has never been amended to reflect the "Christian nation" approach.[15]

The claim is sometimes made that the drafters of the Constitution really intended this to be officially a Christian nation. However, if they had wanted to declare officially that the United States of America was a Christian nation, they likely could have and would have done so. They did not.

If Christianity were somehow to become the official religion of the United States, which form would it be? Episcopal? Congregational? Evangelical? Roman Catholic? Who would determine what *Christian* means? The decision would be up to the government, something the Founding Fathers did not want government to do. Baptists were opposed to any such approach.

Efforts have been made through the years to amend the Constitution to indicate that the United States is officially a Christian nation. For example, the National Reform Association was organized in 1863 with a stated goal "to secure such an amendment to the Constitution of the United States as will declare the nation's allegiance to Jesus Christ and its acceptance of the moral laws of the Christian religion, and so indicate that this is a Christian nation."[16] Similar amendments were still being introduced a hundred years later.[17]

Baptist historian William Estep wrote,

> *It is incredible that after two hundred years of reaping the incalculable benefit of the First Amendment there are Christians who appear determined to eliminate it, if not by a constitutional convention then by reinterpretation. The present assault on the First Amendment, amounts to a siege—a siege based to a large extent upon misunderstanding, misinformation, and/or distortion.*[18]

Apart from a constitutional amendment, the "Christian nation" proponents advocate various matters, such as basing state and national legislation on Christian values; having Christian values taught in the public schools, including devotional Bible reading, prayer, and worship times; and encouraging government leaders to acclaim publicly the United States as a Christian nation. Since many of these practices were present earlier in our country's history when a sort of unofficial "Protestant Establishment" existed, proponents of this view feel the nation has been pulled away from its Christian heritage by alien forces.

Certainly Baptists would rather not have a government that is antagonistic to religion or that is avowedly atheistic. However, most Baptists believe there is only one way to make a nation truly Christian and that is by individuals becoming Christians. A nation is not Christian. People are. Prayer, personal witness, and passionate evangelism provide means for people to become Christians. Passing laws or amending the Constitution will not make people Christians or the nation a Christian nation.

Baptist separationists are not unaware of the relationship of certain Christian values with the founding of the United States. The Founding Fathers were not anti-religious and often spoke favorably of the Christian faith.[19] The Continental Congress in 1774 designated a clergyman to open each session in prayer.[20] The most active advocates of church-state separation, such as Thomas Jefferson and James Madison, were members of the Anglican Church. George Washington began the tradition of using a Bible as part of the presidential inauguration ceremony. The Founding Fathers called for national days of prayer and often declared that the nation enjoyed the benefit of Providence. However, none of this makes the United States officially a "Christian nation."

Baptists have generally accepted, even affirmed, various forms of government acknowledgment of religious heritage. Some have, however, expressed concern that these government expressions of religion contain at least two potential dangers: (1) Advocates of a "Christian nation" approach might claim the government expressions as precedent for more overt government support of religion in general and the Christian faith in particular. (2) Such expressions establish a kind of *civil religion* that could inoculate people from the serious commitment called for by the Lord Jesus Christ (Luke 6:46).

The Nonpreferentialist Approach to Church-State Relations

Proponents of what is called a nonpreferentialist approach profess a belief in religious freedom and do not necessarily oppose separation of church and state. They do, however, disagree with the strict approach to separation.[21]

A basic premise of the nonpreferentialist approach to church-state relations is that the Constitution and the Founding Fathers did not want to exclude the government from promoting religion but wanted only to prevent establishing any one church as the national church or giving any religion preferential treatment. Nonpreferential treatment of churches and religion, according to this view, is not only acceptable under the Constitution but desirable as long as no coercion is involved.

To present this viewpoint as monolithic is not fair. Many variations exist. Advocates propose a variety of ways they believe government can promote religion constitutionally, such as certain forms of vouchers for schools, non-sectarian prayer in public schools and government events, tax funds for church-sponsored charitable efforts, and the display of religious symbols on government property under certain conditions.

For a number of reasons, strict separationists disagree with the nonpreferential interpretation of the Constitution. For example, the Founders were familiar with nonpreferential approaches to church-state relations, and Madison and others adamantly opposed them. In Virginia, Patrick Henry had introduced a General Assessment Bill that would have taxed citizens for the support of religious teachers with the provision that the funds would go to various religious groups. Madison wrote his famous *Memorial and Remonstrance* in opposition to this bill, referring to it as an "establishment of religion."

Baptists in Virginia also strenuously opposed the Henry bill and lobbied against it. They insisted the Bible teaches that the Christian movement is to be financed voluntarily and not by taxation and that government financial support of churches has inevitably led to catastrophe.

In New England, Isaac Backus and other Baptists condemned taxing people for the support of churches. In a sense the tax was nonpreferential in that various religious groups could receive the funds according to the wishes of the populace in each area. Backus argued that such a tax violated the conscience of those opposed to the religion it was used to support and that governments had no right to regulate religious activity.

If the people who drafted the Constitution and the First Amendment had wanted to provide nonpreferential support for religion, they could have done so. But they chose not to do this. Church-state scholar Brent Walker observes, "The weight of history and the plain meaning in the language adopted argue persuasively that the founders rejected any kind of watered-down 'non-preferentialism' and certainly did not intend to establish a Christian theocracy."[22]

However, various people and groups through the years have tried numerous ways to obtain government funds and support for religious activities. Until the past few decades such efforts proved more or less futile. Recently, however, the Supreme Court has more and more leaned toward a nonpreferential approach.

Support of Church-State Separation

Many Baptists and others are aware of challenges to strict but friendly separation of church and state and endeavor to counter them. Here are some of the actions being taken—and that we yet need to take— that are aimed at preserving religious freedom through strict, friendly separation of church and state.

Alert People to the Dangers to Religious Freedom

Historian Glenn Hinson observes that "the most serious danger for religious liberty is *to assume that there is no danger*."[23] Indeed, indifference and apathy define the attitude of many concerning religious freedom and church-state separation.

Another danger is for the nation to embrace an extreme position on church-state relations. In the book *Finding Common Ground* the authors comment:

There are disturbing signs that the American experiment in liberty may
be in danger from two extremes. . . .
   On one end of the political spectrum there are those who seek to
establish in law a 'Christian America.' On the other end are some who
seek to exclude religion from public life entirely. Both proposals violate
the spirit of religious liberty.[24]

Provide Factual Information About the Bases of Religious Freedom

Many people are unaware of the bases for religious freedom and
church-state separation. Recent immigrants and youth are especially
at risk in not knowing the bases for both separation and religious
freedom. Excellent materials are available and ought to be widely dis-
tributed and taught.[25]

Clarify Points of Misinformation

An understanding of the process, reasoning, and beliefs of the
Founding Fathers in drafting the Constitution is important to clarify
misinformation. History is always open to interpretation. However,
most historians agree that the founders intended to establish a nation
that was not hostile to religion but neutral.

To insist that the First Amendment's establishment clause was
meant only to prevent the establishment of a national church and
not to prohibit nonpreferential government funding and support of
religion is a misunderstanding of the Founders' intent. For example,
James Madison, a major contributor to the First Amendment, was
opposed to government funding for religious causes. Later as president of the United States, Madison vetoed bills that would have
benefited both Episcopalians and Baptists financially.[26]

Some contend that "separation of church and state" does not
appear in the Constitution and therefore was not intended by the
Founders. Although the words "separation of church and state" do
not appear in the Constitution, the concept of separation is clear. The
Constitution does not contain a number of words and phrases often
used to describe concepts set forth in it, such as the terms "fair trial,"

"separation of powers," "religious freedom," and "Bill of Rights." This absence does not make such concepts invalid.

Considerable misinformation also surrounds the role of religion in public schools. Some people believe the Supreme Court banned God from public schools by eliminating prayer and by forbidding the reading of the Bible in schools. However, as church-state separationist advocate James Dunn noted, "God has never been absent or tardy from school." The fact is that the Court ruled that *government-drafted and mandated prayer* in schools was unconstitutional. By forbidding such prayers the Court actually enhanced religious freedom since students no longer have to hear government-composed prayer.

Many religious activities are allowed by law in public schools. Some schools overzealously apply the Court's rulings. Continuing clarification is needed as to what is allowable and what is not. Government-sponsored religious activity, especially of a sectarian nature, is not allowed, but much is allowed.[27]

Baptist strict church-state separationists indicate that schools "should accommodate the rights of students to practice their religion in ways that do not disrupt the education process or interfere with the rights of other students not to participate."[28] For example, students can pray silently, form prayer and Bible study clubs, bring Bibles and other religious books to school and read them in off-periods, discuss religion with fellow students, and express religious convictions in school assignments.

What religious expression is allowable under the Constitution in public schools will continue to be debated for years to come. Healthy discussion is needed on the relation of religion and morality in the educational process of public schools, based on a commitment to religious freedom.[29]

The argument that separation of church and state in the United States is hostile to religion is not accurate. The nation's founders, while critical of church-state union, were friendly toward religion. Baptist separationists indicate that religion sometimes deserves and receives some special treatment in order to lift various government-imposed burdens. Examples include zoning for protection of church buildings and discrimination based on religion in hiring people for church positions.[30]

Publicize the Dangers of Government Nonpreferential Support

The nonpreferentialist support of religion, such as providing vouchers for religious schools, can cause numerous problems. Among these are the following concerns:

- It weakens, not strengthens religion. John Leland stated, "Experience, the best teacher, has informed us, that the fondness of magistrates to foster Christianity, has done it more harm than all the persecution ever did."[31]
- It leads to government control. If the government pays for programs by churches, it has a right to control, regulate, and monitor such programs.
- It tends to muzzle the prophetic voice of churches.
- It causes religious groups to de-emphasize their distinctiveness or even their religious nature. In order to secure funds, churches are tempted to emphasize that what they are doing is really secular or generally humanitarian service.
- It requires taxpayers to support religious causes in which they do not believe, thereby violating their religious conscience and freedom.
- It puts the government in the role of determining which religions are worthy of support and which are not. If the support is genuinely nonpreferential, for example, would Baptists be happy with tax support for schools operated by Satanists?
- It puts religious groups in competition with one another for tax support. There is never enough money to satisfy all the requests.
- It opens the door for fraud unless—and even if—the use of funds is monitored closely. Monitoring by the government requires extensive staff and expense.

- It favors religious groups predisposed to seek and accept government funding and discriminates against those whose convictions cause them to reject such funding.
- It results in religious groups becoming more and more dependent on such funding, relying on the authority of government to tax instead of the power of God to provide.

Explain the Meaning of Church-State Separation

Unfortunately, discussions about church-state relations often get hung up on terms such as "wall of separation" or even the word "separation" instead of exploring what is the best relationship between church and state for maximum religious freedom. The word "separation" does have merit in such discussions. What are some of the positive meanings of the term? Here are a few of the things it means that are frequently misunderstood:

Church-state separation allows political activity by Christians and other religious people or groups. The Constitution does not forbid such activity. And Baptists certainly do not believe that such activity is contrary to separation. Baptist historian Estep stated, "The First Amendment did mean to insure the *institutional* separation of church and state. However, it did not intend to disenfranchise Christians or keep them from being the 'salt, light, and leaven' of Christ's vision in any given society."[32]

Separationist Brent Walker observes,

It is difficult to overemphasize the importance of the separation of church and state in protecting religious liberty. But it is equally important to affirm that the institutional separation of church and state does not require a divorcement of religion from politics or relieve Christians from their duties of secular citizenship.[33]

Similarly, James Wood declared, "... So far as the American Constitution is concerned, religion is legally protected to engage in legislative policy advocacy or lobbying to influence any branch or level of government."[34]

Various groups are engaged in political activity from a religious point of view. Freedom of religion affirms their right to do this. However, for Christians to identify and support a particular political party as *the* Christian party is potentially disastrous. For a church to engage in partisan political activity, such as endorsing candidates, carries many risks, including loss of tax exemption.

Church-state separation accepts certain religious expression in public life. Although the nation's founders were opposed to union of church and state, they did not oppose all religious expression in public life. In fact, they officially included certain religious practices but in broad, non-sectarian ways. Baptists in general have not opposed these symbols of religion in national life. However, some have warned about the potential dangers of such "civil religion." [35]

Church-state separation strengthens religion and church life. Separation was viewed by the Founders and by early Baptists as a means of strengthening both religion and government. James Madison, observing the effects of the First Amendment, wrote in 1819 that "the number, industry and morality of the Priesthood, & the devotion of the people have been manifestly increased by the total separation of the Church from the State."[36] Separation of church and state was not designed to either downplay or eliminate religion from American life. Actually, separation frees people from government control to advocate their religious views.

If separation as provided in the Constitution was intended to curtail religion, the effort has been a failure. Religions of all kinds are alive, well, and growing in the United States. America is second to no other nation in the vitality of its religious life. Friendly separation of church and state has allowed Christianity to flourish, using the sword, not of human government (Romans 13:4) but of the Holy Spirit, to empower witnesses (Acts 1:8) and convict people of "guilt in regard to sin" (John 16:8–9).

Champion Freedom in Baptist Life

Baptists led in the struggle for religious freedom and separation of church and state in the United States. If the Baptist voice is muted on these issues, then the risk of erosion in separation is increased. Unfortunately, Baptist voices are heard attacking and belittling separation of church and state.

On the other hand, a resurgence of interest exists among many Baptists in religious freedom and separation of church and state. Believers in church-state separation will not stand silently by while people clip away at Roger Williams's hedge of separation. The hope is that anti-separation expression will be met by a massive chorus by Baptists of praise for religious freedom and friendly separation.

One of the best ways to strengthen freedom in Baptist life and thus in the nation is for Baptists to make responsible use of the freedom that is ours. Baptist pastors, teachers, authors, and other individuals should send forth a barrage of information about religious freedom. Baptist churches, associations, conventions, universities, seminaries, and publishing houses should constantly offer means for people to learn about the importance of religious freedom and the threats to it. Baptists should generously support with prayer, time, and finances those organizations devoted to preserving religious freedom and separation of church and state.

Every Baptist ought to use the freedom inherent in Baptist distinctives in responsible ways and thus strengthen freedom. As Baptist historian Charles Deweese has declared, "Freedom translates into voluntarily accepted accountability, responsibility, and ministry."[37] For example, the freedom to read and interpret the Bible ought to be matched with responsible Bible study and application. The freedom to start churches and proclaim the gospel ought to be matched with responsible effort to launch new churches and enhance evangelistic efforts.

Another aspect of freedom is for Baptists to keep free from the immoral, worldly, and materialistic aspects of culture. Consider this prophetic word: "We are worldly. The world has broken down the wall of separation, of which Roger Williams spoke, and has entered God's garden, and the result is total wilderness. The candlestick has not only gone out, but also its light and warmth are not even missed."[38]

Encourage Religious Freedom Throughout the World

Full religious freedom is actually rare in our world. Religious groups
that imposed heavy persecution on dissenters in the past, such as
the Roman Catholic Church and various Protestant denominations,
have now declared their commitment to religious freedom. However,
various religions and governments still oppose religious freedom
and inflict persecution on religious groups. For example, the United
States Department of State's annual "International Religious Freedom Report" contains an extensive account of the lack of religious
freedom in many nations. It lists five distinct categories of abuse of
religious freedom.[39]

The daily news brings accounts of persecution of people in various countries for their religious views. Baptists in the United States
have a responsibility to help people in other places in the world to
experience the joy of religious freedom found ultimately through
the friendly separation of church and state. One way to do this is by
encouraging and supporting Baptists in other nations as they strive
for freedom. Another way is to urge our government to affirm religious freedom throughout the world.

Conclusion

The struggle for liberty of conscience is an ongoing challenge. The
effort must continue generation after generation, or precious, frail
freedom will be lost. It can be lost both by neglect and by attack.
Therefore, we who are the beneficiaries of freedom must preserve it
by utilizing it, protecting it, and never caving in to those who would
snatch it away. Only then can "the freedom road" be maintained.

And Finally

ACTUALLY THERE IS NO CLOSURE—NO *finally*—to the issue of religious freedom. The issue is too complex to be understood or explored fully. Yet the issue is too important to put aside because of difficulty.

Further, the issue is too dynamic ever to be captured fully. The struggle for religious freedom is ongoing, never complete. Forces are always at work to limit or destroy it. Changes in social structures create constant debate on exactly how religious freedom is to be realized and applied to both church and state.

As history continues, Baptists will persist in making "the freedom road" part of it. Too long have Baptists struggled for religious freedom, too great a price have we paid in that struggle, for us now to sit idly by and allow others who do not have a passion for religious liberty to craft the future. Religious freedom is too much a part of the *Baptist DNA*, too important an ingredient in the Baptist "recipe," too significant a note in the Baptist symphony for it not to remain a priority.

Baptists, when true to their beliefs and heritage, will always support efforts to provide religious liberty for all people. What are the reasons for their unconditional commitment to religious freedom? Baptists look to the Bible for their faith and practice and believe the Bible teaches that religious freedom is a God-given right. Furthermore, Baptists have felt personally the lash of persecution that results from church-state union, and they are familiar with the horrible history of such union. For that additional reason, they stand staunchly for friendly separation of church and state.

In the United States, Baptists have been at the forefront in the effort to establish religious freedom for all. Yet there is always the temptation to rest, to believe the battle has been won, to fool ourselves into believing religious freedom is too firmly entrenched in the

American way of life to be lost. Let us not be deceived. Freedoms of all sorts, and especially religious freedom, are always in peril.

So let us pay whatever price is necessary to protect, preserve, and advance religious freedom for all people today and for the generations to follow. Resist those who would endeavor to establish themselves as the voice of God for others and thus abridge freedom. Reject the intrusion of government into the spiritual affairs of religious institutions. Refuse to use the power of government instead of the power of the Spirit to extend the kingdom of God. Celebrate religious freedom in spite of the challenges associated with it. Tell the story again and again of how religious liberty became a reality.

In 1832 Samuel Smith, a twenty-year-old Baptist seminary student, overwhelmed with a sense of gratitude for freedom in America, penned these lines that have been sung by millions of people over the succeeding years:[1]

> Let music swell the breeze,
> And ring from all the trees,
> Sweet freedom's song;
> Let mortal tongues awake;
> Let all that breathe partake;
> Let rocks their silence break,
> The sound prolong.

May sweet freedom's song ever be sung as we walk "the freedom road"!

Notes

Text of Inscription on Front Cover

1. Previous resources available in this series include the following: *Jesus Is Lord!* by Howard K. Batson; and *The Bible—You Can Believe It* by James C. Denison. Teaching Guides that accompany these books are also available. See the order form at the end of this book. The initial book in this series, *Back to Bedrock: Messages on Our Historic Baptist Faith* by Paul W. Powell is no longer in print.
2. Thomas Helwys (ca.1550-ca.1616), *A Short Declaration of the Mystery of Iniquity 1611/1612*, edited and introduced by Richard Groves (Macon, Georgia: Mercer University Press, 1998), xxiv.

Introduction

1. The terms *religious liberty* and *religious freedom* are used interchangeably in this book. Glenn Hinson provides this definition, using both terms: *"'Religious liberty' means the freedom of every human being, whether as an individual or in a group, from social coercion in religious matters. . . .* Religious liberty defined in this manner encompasses several freedoms. One is freedom of conscience, the right freely to determine what faith or creed one will follow. Others are freedom of religious expression, freedom of association, and freedom for corporate and institutional activities." *Religious Liberty* (Louisville, KY: Glad River, 1991), 13, italics in original.
2. George Bancroft, *History of The United States from The Discovery of the American Continent to The Declaration of Independence* (London: George Routledge and Sons, The Broadway, Ludgate, 1834), 399.
3. Herbert S. Skeats and Charles S. Miall, *History of the Free Churches of England 1688—1891* (London: Alexander & Shepheard, 1891), 19.
4. George C. Lorimer, *The Great Conflict* (Boston: Lee and Shepard, Publishers, 1877), 13.
5. Frank S. Mead, *See These Banners Go* (New York: The Bobbs-Merrill Company, 1936), 97.
6. William Warren Sweet, *The Story of Religion in America* (New York: Harper & Row, 1950), 193.
7. Leo Pfeffer, *Church, State, and Freedom* (Boston: The Beacon Press, 1953), 88.

8. Cited in Charles W. Deweese, *Freedom: The Key to the Baptist Genius* (Brentwood, Tennessee: Baptist History and Heritage Society, 2006), 18.

9. William L. Lumpkin, *Baptist Confessions of Faith,* rev. ed. (Valley Forge: Judson Press, 1969), 140.

10. Thomas Helwys (ca.1550-ca.1616), *A Short Declaration of the Mystery of Iniquity 1611/1612,* edited and introduced by Richard Groves (Macon, Georgia: Mercer University Press, 1998), 53.

11. E. Y. Mullins, *The Axioms of Religion* (Philadelphia: The Griffith & Rowland Press, 1908), 189.

12. George W. Truett, *God's Call to America,* compiled and edited by J. B. Cranfill (Nashville: The Sunday School Board of the Southern Baptist Convention, 1923), 32.

13. For a collection of Baptist confessions see Lumpkin, *Baptist Confessions of Faith,* rev. ed. (Valley Forge: Judson Press, 1969).

14. Cited in original spelling in William L. Lumpkin, *Baptist Confessions of Faith,* rev. ed. 170–171.

15. Article XVII, *The Baptist Faith and Message,* 1963.

Chapter One

1. Isaac Backus, "An Appeal to the Public for Religious Liberty, 1773," in William G. McLoughlin, ed. by, *Isaac Backus on Church, State, and Calvinism, Pamphlets, 1754–1789* (Cambridge, Massachusetts: The Belknap Press of Harvard University Press, 1968), 318.

2. For information on the religious freedom in nations of the world see U. S. Commission on International Religious Freedom (USCIRF), 800 N. Capitol Street, N. W., Suite 790, Washington, D. C., 20002; U.S. Department of State, Bureau of Democracy, Human Rights, and Labor, Office of International Religious Freedom, 2201 C Street N.W., Washington D. C. 20520; Christian Solidarity International, 870 Hampshire Road, Suite T, Westlake Village, CA.

3. James Leo Garrett, Jr., editor-in-chief, *We Baptists* (Franklin, Tennessee: Providence House Publishers, 1999), 38.

4. Thieleman J. van Braght, *The Bloody Theater or Martyrs Mirror of the Defenseless Christians,* compiled from Various Authentic Chronicles, Memorials, and Testimonies, trans. Joseph F. Sohm (Scottdale, Pennsylvania: Herald Press, 1886), 113.

5. Williston Walker and Richard A. Norris, David W. Lotz, Robert T. Handy, *A History of the Christian Church,* 4th ed. (New York: Charles Scribner's Sons, 1985), 125. The *Chi Rho* is one of the earliest symbols used by Christians. It is formed by superimposing the first two letters of the word "Christ" in Greek, chi=ch, and the rho=r. This became the official imperial insignia under Constantine.

6. Walker, *A History of the Christian Church,* 4th ed., 125.

7. Robert A. Baker, *The Baptist March in History* (Nashville: Convention Press, 1958), 15.

8. Bruce L. Shelley, *Church History in Plain Language*, updated 2nd ed. (Nashville: Thomas Nelson Publishers, 1995), 96.

9. Shelley, *Church History in Plain Language*, updated 2nd ed., 96.

10. Walker, *A History of the Christian Church*, 4th ed., 145.

11. Shelley, *Church History in Plain Language*, updated 2nd ed., 96–97.

12. Walker, *A History of the Christian Church*, 4th ed., 197.

13. The term "Middle Ages" has been used by historians to refer to a period somewhere between A.D. 274 and A.D. 1500. Scholars do not agree on the precise dating. Some refer to an Early Middle Ages, Middle Ages, and Later Middle Ages. Historian Sidney Painter states, "But in broad outline tradition has by now sanctified the basic concept of the Middle Ages as the period between ancient and modern times." Sidney Painter, *A History of the Middle Ages, 284–1500* (New York: Alfred A. Knoph, 1954), v.

14. Justo L. González, *The Story of Christianity*, vol. 1, *The Early Church to the Dawn of the Reformation* (New York: HarperSanFrancisco, 1984), 268.

15. Walker, *A History of the Christian Church*, 4th ed., 275–276.

16. Walker, *A History of the Christian Church*, 4th ed., 307.

17. Walker, *A History of the Christian Church*, 4th ed., 309.

18. Matthew 13:24–30 was often used to condemn persecution. For a discussion of various Scriptures used to endorse and condemn persecution see Glenn Hinson, *Religious Liberty* (Louisville: Glad River Publications, 1991), 25–33.

Chapter Two

1. L. F. Greene, ed., *The Writings of the Late Elder John Leland* (New York: G. W. Wood, 1845), 184.

2. Kenneth Scott Latourette, *A History of the Expansion of Christianity*, vol. 2, *The Thousand Years of Uncertainty*, (London: Eyre and Spottiswoode, 1938), 297.

3. Justo L. González, *The Story of Christianity*, vol. 1. *The Early Church to the Dawn of the Reformation* (New York: HarperSanFrancisco, A Division of HarperCollins Publishers, 1984), 293.

4. William R. Estep, *Renaissance and Reformation* (Grand Rapids, Michigan: William B. Eerdmans Publishing Company, 1986), 10.

5. Gonzalez, *The Story of Christianity*, vol. 1, 325.

6. Erasmus was part of the Renaissance commonly referred to as humanism. He was "universally regarded as the prince of humanistic scholars, the dominant figure in the literary world of Europe." Williston Walker and Richard A. Norris, David W. Lotz, Robert T. Handy, *A History of the Christian Church*, 4th ed. (New York: Charles Scribner's Sons, 1985), 409.

7. Bruce L. Shelley, *Church History in Plain Language*, updated 2nd ed. (Nashville: Thomas Nelson Publishers, 1995), 260.

8. Estep, *Renaissance and Reformation*, 316.
9. The term Anabaptists is used for a wide variety of people, including some who were pacifists and others who were military zealots. For an extensive discussion of the Anabaptist movement, see William R. Estep, *The Anabaptist Story*, 3rd ed. (Grand Rapids, Michigan: William B. Eerdmans Publishing Company, 1996) and George Huntston Williams, *The Radical Reformation* (Philadelphia: The Westminster Press, 1962).
10. George Williams, *The Radical Reformation*, 120–127, contains an account of the event and incidents leading up to and following it.
11. Estep, *The Anabaptist Story*, 3rd ed., 14.
12. Estep, *The Anabaptist Story*, 3rd ed., 46.
13. George Williams, *The Radical Reformation*, 145–146.
14. Estep, *The Anabaptist Story*, 3rd ed., 72.
15. Estep, *The Anabaptist Story*, 3rd ed., 97.
16. George Williams, *The Radical Reformation*, 229.
17. George Williams, *The Radical Reformation*, 229.
18. Estep, *The Anabaptist Story*, 3rd ed., 160.
19. Cited in original spelling in William L. Lumpkin, *Baptist Confessions of Faith*, rev. ed. (Valley Forge: Judson Press, 1969), 153.

Chapter Three

1. Thomas Helwys (ca.1550-ca.1615), *A Short Declaration of the Mystery of Iniquity (1611/1612)*, edited and introduced by Richard Groves (Macon, Georgia: Mercer University Press, 1998), 53.
2. Bill J. Leonard, *An Introduction to Baptist Principles* (Brentwood, Tennessee: Baptist History and Heritage Society, 2005), 20.
3. G. Hugh Wamble, "Baptist Contributions to Separation of Church and State," *Baptist History and Heritage*, 20, no. 3 (July, 1985): 3.
4. H. Leon McBeth, *A Sourcebook for Baptist Heritage* (Nashville: Broadman Press, 1990), 70.
5. William R. Estep, *Revolution Within the Revolution, The First Amendment in Historical Context, 1612–1789* (Grand Rapids, Michigan: William B. Eerdmans Publishing Company, 1990), 46, italics in original.
6. Another early Baptist book on religious freedom was by Mark Leonard Busher, *Religion's Peace: Or a Plea for Liberty of Conscience*. See Estep, *Revolution Within the Revolution*, 55–62. Others were written by John Murton.
7. Estep, *Revolution Within the Revolution*, 52.
8. King James I believed himself to be the ruler of both church and state. His desire for religious unity led him to commission a translation of the Bible to be read in all of the worship services of England. It is known today as the King James Version of the Bible or the Authorized Version; it was authorized by the king who arrested and imprisoned the first Baptist pastor of England.

9. William H. Brackney, ed., *Baptist Life and Thought, A Source Book*, rev. ed., (Valley Forge: Judson Press, 1998), 77.

10. E. Glenn Hinson, *Religious Liberty* (Louisville: Glad River Publications, 1991), 95.

11. E. Y. Mullins, *The Axioms of Religion* (Philadelphia: The Griffith & Rowland Press, 1908), 189–190.

12. Jon Meacham, *American Gospel* (New York: Random House, 2006), 43.

13. Edwin S. Gaustad and Leigh E. Schmidt, *The Religious History of America*, rev. ed. (New York: HarperSanFrancisco, 2002), 53.

14. William Warren Sweet, *The Story of Religion in America*, rev. and enlarged ed. (New York: Harper & Brothers Publishers, 1950), 51.

15. Roland H. Bainton, *The Travail of Religious Liberty, Nine Biographical Studies* (Philadelphia: The Westminster Press, 1951), 212.

16. Sweet, *The Story of Religion in America*, rev. and enlarged ed., 51.

17. Edwin S. Gaustad, *Liberty of Conscience: Roger Williams in America* (Grand Rapids, Michigan: William B. Eerdmans Publishing Company, 1999), 56.

18. Cited in Sweet, *The Story of Religion in America*, rev. and enlarged ed., 71, regular type indicates italics in original.

19. Roger Williams, "Mr. Cotton's Letter Lately Printed, Examined and Answered," in *The Complete Writings of Roger Williams*, vol. 1, ed. Perry Miller (New York: Russell and Russell, Inc., 1963; reprinted by Baptist Standard Bearer, 2005), 108.

20. Some historians credit this as being the first Baptist church established in America.

21. John Clarke, *Ill Newes from New England* (London: Henry Hills, 1652), reprinted in original form by The Baptist Standard Bearer, Inc., 8.

22. Louis Franklin Asher, *John Clarke (1609–1676): Pioneer in American Medicine, Democratic Ideals, and Champion of Religious Liberty* (Pittsburg: Dorrance Publishing Co., Inc, 1997), 77.

23. William H. Brackney, *The Baptists* (Westport, CT: Praeger Publishers, 1994), 95.

24. McBeth, *A Sourcebook for Baptist Heritage*, 83.

25. Brackney, *The Baptists*, 93.

26. Isaac Backus, *History of New England with Particular Reference to the Denomination of Christians Called Baptists*, 2nd ed. with Notes by David Weston, vol. I. (Newton, Mass: The Backus Historical Society, 1871), reprinted in original form by The Baptist Standard Bearer, Inc., Paris, Arkansas, 197.

27. Clarke, *Ill Newes from New England*, 50–51.

28. Asher, *John Clarke (1609–1676): Pioneer in American Medicine, Democratic Ideals, and Champion of Religious Liberty*, 64. This book provides an analysis of the setting for and the results of the persecution of Clarke, Holmes, and Crandall.

29. Although all Baptists believed passionately in religious freedom and realized that this called for church and state to be separate, they differed on the degree and nature of the separation. For example, John Leland and Isaac Backus differed somewhat in their views. For a succinct discussion of these differences see Albert W. Wardin, Jr., "Contrasting Views for Church and State: A Study of John Leland and Isaac Backus," *Baptist History and Heritage*, 33, no. 1 (Winter, 1998): 12–20.

30. Estep, *Revolution Within the Revolution*, 112.

31. Thomas J. Curry, *The First Freedoms* (New York: Oxford University Press, 1986), 131.

32. Isaac Backus, *History of New England with Particular Reference to the Denomination of Christians Called Baptists*, vol. 2, 98–99.

33. William G. McLoughlin, ed., *Isaac Backus on Church, State, and Calvinism: Pamphlets, 1754–1789* (Cambridge, Massachusetts: The Belknap Press of Harvard University Press, 1968), 342, italics in original.

34. William G. McLoughlin, *Isaac Backus and the American Pietistic Tradition*, ed. Oscar Handlin (Boston: Little, Brown and Company, 1967), 127.

35. Brackney, *The Baptists*, 98.

36. McLoughlin, *Issac Backus and the American Pietistic Tradition*, 132.

37. Curry, *The First Freedoms*, 1986), 182.

38. Richard B. Cook, *The Story of the Baptists in All Ages and Countries* (Dallas and Galveston: Thayer & Hewlett, 1886), 224.

39. O.K. and Marjorie Armstrong, *Baptists Who Shaped A Nation* (Nashville: Broadman Press, 1975), 18.

40. Garnett Ryland, *The Baptists of Virginia 1699–1926* (Richmond: The Virginia Baptist Board of Missions and Education, 1955), 64–65.

41. L. F. Green, ed., *The Writings of the Late Elder John Leland* (New York: G. W. Wood, 1845; reprint, New York: Arno Press, 1970), 184.

42. Ryland, *The Baptists of Virginia 1699–1926*, 166–168.

43. Gaustad, *Liberty of Conscience: Roger Williams in America*, x.

Chapter Four

1. Slayden A. Yarbrough, "Church and State in Baptist History," *Baptist History and Heritage*, 33, no. 1 (Winter, 1998): 9.

2. Thomas Helwys (ca.1550-ca.1616), *A Short Declaration of the Mystery of Iniquity 1611/1612*, edited and introduced by Richard Groves (Macon, Georgia: Mercer University Press, 1998), 62.

3. George W. Truett, *God's Call to America*, compiled and edited by J. B. Cranfill (Nashville: The Sunday School Board of the Southern Baptist Convention, 1923), 43.

4. See T. B. Maston, *Christianity and World Issues* (New York: The Macmillan Company, 1957), 216.

5. Truett, *God's Call to America*, 32–33.
6. E. Glenn Hinson, *Religious Liberty* (Louisville: Glad River Publications, 1991), 103.
7. Louis Franklin Asher, *John Clarke (1609–1676): Pioneer in American Medicine, Democratic Ideals, and Champion of Religious Liberty* (Pittsburgh: Dorrance Publishing, Inc. 1997), 77.
8. Cited in original spelling in Asher, *John Clarke (1609–1676), Pioneer in American Medicine, Democratic Ideal, and Champion of Religious Liberty*, 77.
9. Asher, *John Clarke (1609–1676): Pioneer in American Medicine, Democratic Ideals, and Champion of Religious Liberty*, 78.
10. Garnett Ryland, *The Baptists of Virginia 1699–1926* (Richmond: The Virginia Baptist Board of Missions and Education, 1955), 128.
11. Roger Williams, "Mr. Cotton's Letter Lately Printed, Examined and Answered," in *The Complete Writings of Roger Williams*, vol. 1, ed. Perry Miller (New York: Russell and Russell, Inc., 1963; reprinted by Baptist Standard Bearer, 2005), 108.
12. Mark DeWolfe Howe, *The Garden and The Wilderness* (Chicago: The University of Chicago Press, 1965), 6–7.
13. Ryland, *The Baptists of Virginia 1699–1926*, 128–129.
14. William G. McLoughlin, *Issac Backus and the American Pietistic Tradition*, ed. Oscar Handlin (Boston: Little, Brown and Company, 1967), 122.
15. Walter B. Shurden, *The Baptist Identity* (Macon, Georgia: Smyth & Helwys Publishing, Inc., 1993), 49.
16. John Witte, Jr., *Religion and the American Constitutional Experiment*, 2nd ed. (Boulder, Colorado: Westview Press, 2005), 190.
17. William Taylor Thom, *The Struggle for Religious Freedom in Virginia: The Baptists* (Baltimore: John Hopkins Press, 1900), 78, cited in Ryland, *The Baptists of Virginia 1699–1926*, 126.
18. Lenni Brenner, ed., *Jefferson & Madison on Separation of Church and State* (Fort Lee, New Jersey: Barricade Books, 2004), 345.
19. Roger Williams, *The Bloudy Tenent of Persecution*, cited in Hinson, *Religious Liberty* , 104.
20. John B.Turpin, *A Brief History of the Albemarle Baptist Association*, cited in Ryland, *The Baptists of Virginia 1699–1926*, 169.
21. Daniel L. Dreisbach, *Thomas Jefferson and the Wall of Separation between Church and State* (New York: New York University Press, 2002), 33–54. This reference contains the multiple drafts of the letter and an analysis of it.
22. Ryland, *The Baptists of Virginia 1699–1926*, 166–168.
23. Leonard W. Levy, *The Establishment Clause* (Chapel Hill, North Carolina: The University of North Carolina Press, 1994), 250. Levy is Andrew W. Mellon All-Claremont Professor Emeritus of Humanities at the Claremont Graduate School. He is editor of the *Encylopedia of the American Constitution*.
24. Ryland, *The Baptists of Virginia 1699–1926*, 134.

25. Richard Labunski, *James Madison and the Struggle for the Bill of Rights* (New York: Oxford University Press, Inc., 2006), 44.

26. Historians debate whether such a meeting took place, but strong evidence exists that it did. See Robert S. Alley, ed., *James Madison on Religious Liberty* (Amherst, New York: Prometheus Books, 1985), 185.

27. Ryland, *The Baptists of Virginia 1699–1926*, 134.

28. William R. Estep, *Revolution Within the Revolution: The First Amendment in Historical Context, 1612–1789* (Grand Rapids, Michigan: William B. Eerdmans Publishing Company, 1990), 167.

29. William G. McLoughlin, *Issac Backus and the American Pietistic Tradition*, 196–201.

30. Robert A. Baker, *A Baptist Source Book* (Nashville: Broadman Press, 1966), 44, italics and capitalization in original; regular type indicates italics in original.

31. Ryland, *The Baptists of Virginia 1699–1926*, 137, italics in original.

32. Labunski, *James Madison and the Struggle for the Bill of Rights*, 159.

33. Labunski, *James Madison and the Struggle for the Bill of Rights*, 162.

34. Brenner, ed., *Jefferson & Madison on Separation of Church and State*, 103–104.

35. Labunski, *James Madison and the Struggle for the Bill of Rights*, 167.

36. Labunski, *James Madison and the Struggle for the Bill of Rights*, 144.

37. Labunski, *James Madison and the Struggle for the Bill of Rights*, 165.

38. Estep, *Revolution Within the Revolution*, 168.

39. Numerous books about various interpretations of religious freedom and separation of church and state have been written. For a list of books from the Baptist separationist position contact the Baptist Joint Committee for Religious Liberty, 200 Maryland Ave. N.E., Washington, D. C. 20002. See also www.bjcpa.org.

40. C. Emanuel Carlson, "The Meaning of Religious Liberty" in James E. Wood, Jr., ed., *Baptists and the American Experience* (Valley Forge: Judson Press, 1976), 203.

41. Carlson, "The Meaning of Religious Liberty," in Wood, *Baptists and the American Experience*, 206. italics in original.

42. Barbara M. Cross, ed., *The Autobiography of Lyman Beecher*, vol. 1 (Cambridge, Massachusetts: The Belknap Press of Harvard University Press, 1961), 252–253, regular type indicates italics in original.

43. Derek H. Davis, edited with an introduction by, *The Separation of Church And State Defended: Selected Writings of James E. Wood, Jr.* (Baylor University, Waco: J. M. Dawson Institute of Church-State Studies, 1995), 54.

44. James Madison, *James Madison Writings* (New York: The Library of America, 1999), 726–727.

45. Samuel Smith, "My Country, 'Tis of Thee."

Chapter Five

1. Edgar Young Mullins, *The Axioms of Religion* (Philadelphia: The Griffith & Rowland Press, 1908), 197.
2. Leo Pfeffer, *Church, State, and Freedom* (Boston: The Beacon Press, 1953), 604.
3. William H. Brackney, ed., *Baptist Life and Thought, A Source Book*, rev. ed. (Valley Forge: Judson Press, 1998), 425.
4. John F. Wilson and Donald L. Drakeman, eds., *Church and State in American History*, 3rd ed. expanded and updated (Cambridge, MA: Westview Press, 2003), vii.
5. Winnifred Fallers Sullivan, *The Impossibility of Religious Freedom* (Princeton: Princeton University Press, 2005), 150.
6. For a discussion of new religions and church-state issues, see Derek H. Davis and Barry Hankins, eds., *New Religious Movements and Religious Liberty in America*, 2nd ed. (Baylor University Press: Waco, 2003).
7. The pledge as originally written by a Baptist pastor in 1892 did not contain the words "under God."
8. Words by Julia Ward Howe.
9. William R. Estep, *Revolution Within the Revolution, The First Amendment in Historical Context, 1612–1789* (Grand Rapids, Michigan: William B. Eerdmans Publishing Company, 1990), 178–179.
10. James E. Wood, Jr., E. Bruce Thompson, Robert T. Miller, *Church and State in Scripture, History and Constitutional Law* (Waco: Baylor University Press, 1958), 90.
11. Thomas J. Curry, *The First Freedoms* (New York: Oxford University Press, 1986), 193.
12. Some anti-separationists insist that the Fourteenth Amendment should not have applied the First Amendment to the states and that this was a wrong decision by the Court. However, the First Amendment is now seen as applying to state as well as national law.
13. Wood, Thompson, Miller, *Church and State in Scripture, History and Constitutional Law*, 120–121, citing *Cantwell v. Connecticut*.
14. John T. Noonan, Jr. and Edward McGlynn Gaffney, Jr., *Religious Freedom: History, Cases, and Other Materials on the Interaction of Religion and Government* (New York: Foundation Press, 2001, xi.
15. Unpublished paper in file of J. Brent Walker.
16. J. Brent Walker, *Religious Liberty and Church-State Separation* (Brentwood, Tennessee: Baptist History and Heritage Society, 2003), 24–25, italics in original.
17. Some have argued that James Madison's initial draft of the First Amendment indicated only that he wanted no national church to be established. However, Madison's writings and his acts as president of the United States indicate he intended far more than to prevent the establishment of a national church.

18. Noonan and Gaffney, *Religious Freedom: History, Cases, and Other Materials on the Interaction of Religion and Government*, xi.

19. Wood, Thompson, Miller, *Church and State in Scripture, History and Constitutional Law*, 144.

20. Elwyn A. Smith, *Religious Liberty in the United States* (Philadelphia: Fortress Press, 1972), 252. Smith discusses the ruling in which this sentence is found. Smith also points out, "The phrase 'wall of separation of church and state' first appeared in the Supreme Court's opinion in 1879 in *Reynolds v. United States* when Jefferson's celebrated letter to the Baptists of Danbury was quoted." Smith, 253.

21. The Lemon Test, based on a 1971 case of *Lemon v. Kurtzman*, indicated that the Court would rule a practice unconstitutional if it lacked any legitimate secular purpose, had the primary effect of either promoting or inhibiting religion, or excessively entangled government with religion. The Coercion Test, based on the 1992 case of *Lee v. Weisman* indicated that a religious practice was to be examined to see whether any pressure was applied to force people to participate; the Court has defined that such force or coercion occurs when the government directs a formal religious exercise in a way to oblige the participation of objectors. The Endorsement Test indicated that the practice in question is to be examined to determine whether it unconstitutionally endorses religion by conveying a message that religion or a particular religious belief is favored or promoted over other beliefs.

22. Wood, Thompson, Miller, *Church and State in Scripture, History and Constitutional Law*, 91.

23. Ronald B. Flowers, *That Godless Court?*, 2nd ed. (Louisville: Westminster John Knox Press, 2005), 161–162.

24. Anson Phelps Stokes and Leo Pfeffer, *Church and State in the United States*, rev. one-volume ed. (New York: Harper & Row, Publishers, 1964), 147.

25. Flowers, *That Godless Court?*, 160.

26. James Madison, *James Madison Writings* (New York: The Library of America, 1999), 421–422. "Chiefly" is "cheifly" in original.

27. *McCreary County v. A.C.L.U. of Kentucky*, 2005.

Chapter Six

1. William R. Estep, *Why Baptists?* (Dallas: Baptist General Convention of Texas, 1997), 41.

2. J. Brent Walker, *Religious Liberty and Church-State Separation* (Brentwood, Tennessee: Baptist History and Heritage Society, 2003), 7.

3. "I believe in God the Father Almighty, Maker of heaven and earth. And in Jesus Christ his only Son our Lord; who was conceived by the Holy Ghost, born of the Virgin Mary, suffered under Pontius Pilate, was crucified, dead, and buried; he descended into hell; the third day he rose again from the dead; he ascended into heaven, and sitteth on the right hand of

God the Father Almighty; from thence he shall come to judge the quick and the dead. I believe in the Holy Ghost; the holy catholic Church; the communion of saints; the forgiveness of sins; the resurrection of the body; and the life everlasting."

4. For a discussion of this matter, see D. H. Williams, *The Free Church and the Early Church* (Grand Rapids, Michigan: William B. Eerdmans Publishing Company, 2002).

5. George W. Truett, *God's Call to America*, compiled and edited by J. B. Cranfill (Nashville: The Sunday School Board of the Southern Baptist Convention, 1923), 34. See Howard K. Batson, *Jesus Is Lord* (Dallas: BaptistWay Press, 2006) for a discussion of the Lordship of Christ.

6. William H. Brackney, *The Baptists* (Westport, CT: Praeger Publishers, 1994), 36. See James C. Denison, *The Bible—You Can Believe It* (Dallas: BaptistWay Press, 2005) for a discussion of the Bible as authority.

7. Thomas Helwys (ca.1550-ca.1615), *A Short Declaration of the Mystery of Iniquity (1611/1612)*, edited and introduced by Richard Groves (Macon, Georgia: Mercer University Press, 1998), 53.

8. Truett, *God's Call to America*, 40.

9. Paul Powell, *Back to Bedrock* (Dallas: BaptistWay Press, 2003), Appendix: Articles of Faith, Art. 3, 8.

10. Edgar Young Mullins, *The Axioms of Religion* (Philadelphia: The Griffith & Rowland Press, 1908), 57.

11. H. Leon McBeth, "God Gives Soul Competency and Priesthood to All Believers," *Defining Baptist Convictions*, compiled and edited by Charles W. Deweese (Franklin, Tennessee: Providence House Publishers, 1996), 63.

12. Herschel H. Hobbs, *The Baptist Faith and Message*, rev. ed. (Nashville: Convention Press, 1971), 12.

Chapter Seven

1. John Clarke, *Ill Newes from New England* (London: Henry Hills, 1652; reprinted in original form by The Baptist Standard Bearer, Inc.), 104.

2. *The Baptist Faith and Message*, 1963, Article VI.

3. Matters such as zoning restrictions may affect church meeting places, however.

4. Baptists are aware that some other Christians interpret the Bible differently in regard to church governance and defend their right to act in accord with their beliefs.

5. William R. Estep, *Revolution Within the Revolution: The First Amendment in Historical Context, 1612–1789* (Grand Rapids, Michigan: William B. Eerdmans Publishing Company, 1990), xvii.

6. Billy Graham, *World Aflame* (Garden City, New York: Doubleday and Company, 1965), 187.

Chapter Eight

1. Herschel H. Hobbs, *The Baptist Faith and Message*, rev. ed. (Nashville: Convention Press, 1971), 124.

2. Robert Boston, *Why the Religious Right Is Wrong about Separation of Church & State*, 2nd ed. (New York: Prometheus Books, 2003), 14.

3. Boston, *Why the Religious Right Is Wrong about Separation of Church & State*, 14. See Philip Hamburger, *Separation of Church and State* (Cambridge, Massachusetts: Harvard University Press, 2002).

4. *Wallace v. Jaffree.*

5. Estep, *Revolution Within the Revolution: The First Amendment in Historical Context, 1612–1789* (Grand Rapids, Michigan: William B. Eerdmans Publishing Company, 1990), 9.

6. Derek H. Davis, ed., *The Separation of Church And State Defended: Selected Writings of James E. Wood, Jr.* (Baylor University, Waco: J. M. Dawson Institute of Church-State Studies, 1995), 219.

7. Rousas John Rushdoony, *The Institutes of Biblical Law* (n.p.: The Presbyterian and Reformed Publishing Company, 1973), 20.

8. Rushdoony, *The Institutes of Biblical Law*, 9–10.

9. H. Wayne House and Thomas Ice, *DominionTheology: Blessing or Curse?* (Portland, Oregon: Multnomah Press, 1988), 16.

10. Davis, *The Separation of Church And State Defended: Selected Writings of James E. Wood, Jr.*, 37.

11. Tim LaHaye, *Faith of Our Founding Fathers* (Brentwood, Tennessee: Wolgemuth & Hyatt, Publishers, Inc., 1987), 68.

12. David Barton, *Original Intent*, 3rd ed. (Aledo, Texas: WallBuilder Press, 2004), 150.

13. Barton, *Original Intent*, 3rd ed., 247.

14. J. W. Peltason, *Understanding the Constitution* (New York: Holt, Rinehart and Winston, 1949), 1.

15. Those who insist the Founders did not intend for the United States to be officially a Christian nation also cite various sources for their position. For example a 1797 treaty initiated under President Washington and officially adopted by the Senate under President John Adams specifically states that "the government of the United States of America is not in any sense founded on the Christian Religion." Cited in Jon Meacham, *American Gospel* (New York: Random House, 2006), 262.

16. Boston, *Why the Religious Right Is Wrong about Separation of Church & State*, 103.

17. Boston, *Why the Religious Right Is Wrong about Separation of Church & State*, 104.

18. William R. Estep, *Revolution Within the Revolution:The First Amendment in Historical Context, 1612–1789*, 1–2.

19. Leaders such as Thomas Jefferson and Benjamin Franklin expressed belief in God and affirmed the moral teachings of Jesus but questioned the divinity of Christ. Edwin S. Gaustad, *Faith of the Founders: Religion and the New Nation 1776–1826* (Waco, Texas: Baylor University Press, 2004), 65–66, 100–101.

20. He later resigned, joined the British, and left for England. Delegates to the Constitutional Convention rejected Benjamin Franklin's suggestion that they have prayer.

21. For a succinct summary from a self-professed accomodationist of this view, see Will Dodson, "Church and State in Contemporary United States: Toward a Greater Union: The Accommodation Position," *Baptist History and Heritage*, 33, no. 1 (Winter, 1998): 43–53. Information on the accommodation position (known by various terms, such as the principled pluralism position or nonpreferentialist position) is available from the Ethics and Religious Liberty Commission, 901 Commerce Street, Suite 50, Nashville, Tennessee 37203.

22. J. Brent Walker, *Religious Liberty and Church-State Separation* (Brentwood, Tennessee: Baptist History and Heritage Society, 2003), 16.

23. Hinson, *Religious Liberty* (Louisville: Glad River Publications, 1991), 131, italics in original.

24. Charles C. Haynes and Oliver Thomas, *Finding Common Ground: A Guide to Religious Liberty in Public Schools* (Nashville: First Amendment Center, 2003), 34.

25. Materials and lists of resources from a Baptist separationist point of view are available from The Baptist Joint Committee for Religious Liberty, 200 Maryland Ave. N. E., Washington, D. C. 20002; The Baptist History and Heritage Society, 3001 Mercer University Drive, Atlanta, Georgia 30341; The J. M. Dawson Institute of Church-State Studies and the J. M. Dawson Church-State Research Center, Baylor University, Waco, Texas 76798-7308; the Christian Life Commission, 333 North Washington, Dallas, Texas 75246; The Center for Baptist Studies of Mercer University, 1400 Coleman Avenue, Macon, Georgia, 31207.

26. Leo Pfeffer, *Church, State, and Freedom* (Boston: The Beacon Press, 1953), 140.

27. Information on the numerous religious practices allowable in schools can be obtained from "Guidance on Constitutionally Protected Prayer in Public Elementary and Secondary Schools" issued by the United States Department of Education, 400 Maryland Avenue S.W., Washington, D. C., 20202, and from Charles C. Haynes and Oliver Thomas, *Finding Common Ground: A Guide to Religious Liberty in Public Schools* (Nashville: First Amendment Center, 2003).

28. Walker, *Religious Liberty and Church-State Separation*, 37.

29. See for example James W. Fraser, *Between Church and State* (New York: St. Martin's Press, 1999) and Martin E. Marty with Jonathan Moore, *Education, Religion, and the Common Good* (San Francisco: Jossey-Bass, 2000).

30. Walker, *Religious Liberty and Church-State Separation*, 23–24.

31. L. F. Greene, ed., *The Writings of the Late Elder John Leland* (New York: G. W. Wood, 1845; reprint, New York: Arno Press, 1970), 278.

32. Estep, *Revolution Within the Revolution*, 16, italics in original.

33. Walker, *Religious Liberty and Church-State Separation*, 17.

34. Davis, *The Separation of Church And State Defended: Selected Writings of James E. Wood, Jr.*, 186–187.

35. Robert N. Bellah, a sociologist, in an article entitled "Civil Religion in America" stated, "There actually exists alongside of and rather clearly differentiated from the churches an elaborate and well-institutionalized civil religion. . . ." In William G. McLoughlin and Robert N. Bellah, ed., *Religion in America* (Boston: Houghton Mifflin Company, 1968), 3. Baptist leader Welton Gaddy observes, "Definitions of civil religion are about as numerous as are those people who have written on the subject." In a chapter entitled "One Nation Under God," in James E. Wood, Jr., ed. *Baptists and the American Experience* (Valley Forge: Judson Press, 1976), 120. This chapter and one on "Nationalism and Christian Allegiance" in the same book provide a summary and evaluation of "civil religion."

36. James Madison, *James Madison's Writings* (New York: The Library of America, 1999), 727.

37. Charles Deweese, *Freedom: The Key to the Baptist Genius* (Brentwood, Tennessee: Baptist History and Heritage Society, 2006), 5.

38. Wood, *Baptists and the American Experience*, 211.

39. An annual international religious freedom report is available from the United States Department of State, Bureau for Democracy, Human Rights, and Labor, Office of International Religious Freedom, 2201 C Street N. W., Washington D. C. 20520 and on the website of the Department of State.

And Finally

1. "My Country, 'Tis of Thee."

How to Order More Study Materials

It's easy! Just fill in the following information. For additional Bible study materials, see www.baptistwaypress.org or get a complete order form of available materials by calling 1–866–249–1799 or e-mailing baptistway@bgct.org.

Title of item	Price	Quantity	Cost
This Study:			
Baptists and Religious Liberty (BWP001028)	$6.95	_____	_____
Baptists and Religious Liberty—Large Print (BWP001059)	$8.95	_____	_____
Baptists and Religious Liberty: Teaching Guide (BWP001029)	$1.95	_____	_____
Baptists and Religious Liberty: PowerPoint® CD (BWP001030)	$1.95	_____	_____
Los Bautistas y la Libertad de Religión (BWP001063)	$6.95	_____	_____
Additional Baptist Doctrine and Heritage studies			
Jesus Is Lord! (BWP001011)	$5.95	_____	_____
Jesus Is Lord!—Teaching Guide (BWP001012)	$1.95	_____	_____
The Bible—You Can Believe It (BWP000089)	$4.95	_____	_____
The Bible—You Can Believe It: Teaching Guide (BWP000090)	$1.95	_____	_____
Beliefs Important to Baptists			
Beliefs Important to Baptists—Study Guide (one-volume edition; includes all lessons) (BWP000021)	$2.35	_____	_____
Beliefs Important to Baptists—Teaching Guide (one-volume edition; includes all lessons) (BWP000022)	$1.95	_____	_____
Who in the World Are Baptists, Anyway? (one lesson) (BWP000094)	$ .45	_____	_____
Who in the World Are Baptists, Anyway?—Teacher's Edition (BWP000095)	$ .55	_____	_____
Beliefs Important to Baptists: I (four lessons) (BWP000019)	$1.35	_____	_____
Beliefs Important to Baptists: I—Teacher's Edition (BWP000020)	$1.75	_____	_____
Beliefs Important to Baptists: II (four lessons) (BWP000017)	$1.35	_____	_____
Beliefs Important to Baptists: II—Teacher's Edition (BWP000018)	$1.75	_____	_____
Beliefs Important to Baptists: III (four lessons) (BWP000015)	$1.35	_____	_____
Beliefs Important to Baptists: III—Teacher's Edition (BWP000016)	$1.75	_____	_____
For Children			
Let's Explore Baptist Beliefs (BWP000027)	$3.95	_____	_____
Let's Explore Baptist Beliefs—Leader's Guide (BWP000028)	$2.95	_____	_____

Standard (UPS/Mail) Shipping Charges*	
Order Value	Shipping charge
$.01–$9.99	$6.00
$10.00–$19.99	$7.00
$20.00–$39.99	$8.00
$40.00–$79.99	$9.00
$80.00–$99.99	$12.00
$100.00–$129.99	$14.00
$130.00–$149.99	$18.00
$150.00–$199.99	$21.00
$200.00–$299.99	$26.00
$300.00 and up	10% of order value

Cost of items (Order value) _____
Shipping charges (see chart*) _____
TOTAL _____

*Plus, applicable taxes for individuals and other taxable entities (not churches) within Texas will be added. Please call 1–866–249–1799 if the exact amount is needed prior to ordering.

Please allow three weeks for standard delivery. For express shipping service: Call 1–866–249–1799 for information on additional charges.

YOUR NAME   PHONE

YOUR CHURCH   DATE ORDERED

MAILING ADDRESS

CITY   STATE   ZIP CODE

MAIL this form with your check for the total amount to:

BAPTISTWAY PRESS
Baptist General Convention of Texas
333 North Washington
Dallas, TX 75246-1798

(Make checks to "Baptist Executive Board.")

OR, **FAX** your order anytime to: 214-828-5376, and we will bill you.

OR, **CALL** your order toll-free: 1-866-249-1799
(M-Th 8:30 a.m.–6:00 p.m.; Fri 8:30 a.m.–5:00 p.m. central time),
and we will bill you.

OR, **E-MAIL** your order to our internet e-mail address:
baptistway@bgct.org, and we will bill you.

OR, ORDER **ONLINE** at www.baptistwaypress.org.

We look forward to receiving your order! Thank you!